Young Professional's Handbook

Young Professional's Handbook

© 2021 by Garric Baker. All rights reserved.

Published by Garric Baker

ISBN: 978-0-578-97535-1 (Paperback)

Editing by: Crystal Lenz Editing, Manhattan, Kansas

Cover Design: Garric Baker

i

Acknowledgments

"If I have seen further, it is by standing on the shoulders of giants."

Sir Isaac Newton first penned these words in 1675 in a letter to an acquaintance, Robert Hook. Since, his words echoed throughout the centuries. It is my hope that the following chapters provide you with a metaphorical set of shoulders for you to stand upon to see further. My mission is to create a foundation built upon hundreds of hours of research and several past publications that combines years of experience and education into a few simple pages.

By training, I am an architect; it's a profession that requires lengthy post-secondary education and often a graduate degree. In my education, I attended Kansas State University's College of Architecture, Planning, and Design, graduating in 2013 with a Master of Architecture. As you will learn within this writing, students who endeavor in years-long projects gain a unique outlook when planning their careers. Following graduation, the real work began where I recorded over 5,000 Intern Development Program hours and passed the licensure exam – an exam that consists of six individual three-and-one-half to four-hour components covering a wide array of topics within the architectural field. Upon completion of my education, IDP hours, and successful exams, I was able to call myself a licensed architect. According to the American Association of Architects (AIA), this entire process takes, on average, twelve years to attain. However, I had the unique opportunity to do so while building a portfolio of nearly $27 million in built work, trained eight interns, and negotiated the beginning stages of purchasing the firm I worked for within thirteen years.

Architects not only design commercial buildings and residential projects; we also uniquely design our careers. I have worked on projects that have taken upwards of four- to five-years to implement from concept to completion. These long, sometimes arduous projects take methodical planning, constant evaluation, filing away mental notes for months or years, and driving oneself to pull all the components together into a holistic outcome. Our profession is one that we design buildings while designing our careers. In navigating my career design, I hope to share my efforts through this handbook to help readers design their own careers.

Before we begin, I would like to point out the influential giants within my life and career. It is through their investment and teachings that I have been able to accelerate my career. As a sophomore in high school, standing in front of a panel of interviewers, the following question began my thinking in terms of the work done before me to establish my path: "If I have seen further, it is by standing on the shoulders of giants. What does this famous quote mean to you?"

I proceeded to explain who my personal giants are, firstly, my mother and father. My mother, prior to her retirement, had dedicated her career to a lifetime of teaching kindergarten through sixth-grade special education. I witnessed through her teachings that we all can learn – we simply learn at our own pace and in our own ways. I had unique relationships with her students; where others saw disabilities, I saw others that were my age and just thought a little differently than I did. My father started as a welder the day after high school graduation and continues to do so forty years later. During his career, he was promoted to a group leader and has had several employees under him. One summer, he had an employee, 'Andrew,' who would avoid his responsibilities and instead spend his time being occupied by his cellphone. My father would come home at the end of the day, irritated that the individual would rather be on his cellphone instead of performing the duties required of him. My father would remark, "*if someone pays you to do a job, pick up a broom and sweep, do something – you're there to do a job, you're there getting paid to do a job.*" Those words would remain with me through the early years of my career, knowing that there would be no job above nor beneath me – you can strive to be ambitious and conquer any task but never be too proud to pick up a broom and sweep.

Both parents provided my sister and me with a healthy, humble childhood. They never changed jobs or employment (by choice or otherwise) but continued to their paths and worked committed to providing for their family and striving to better themselves through their work. My older sister often got into trouble for this or that, and I being the younger of the two, watched quietly and learned what was acceptable or not. She too has worked to provide the same childhood for her son that she and I experienced.

Following immediate family, I owe a great deal to my college classmates. I was often envious when professors would comment or praise their work instead of mine; however, then I came to the realization that if I could do just as well as my classmates, then simply just do it! They have made me better without even knowing it, but their striving increased my own striving, and I will forever be grateful for my college 'family.'

After college, I was hired at an architectural firm that had been established thirty years ago and remained under the tutelage of one man for its entirety. He has provided me with the opportunity to engage with the community and the business world, all while allowing me to pursue my employee development as a young professional. His peers would say that I learned to be a professional because I had the most professional employer. He has received awards for being Citizen of the Year in three local cities, Volunteer of the Year in one, and resume of committees and boards a mile-long. He has been, and remains, admired by his peers because of his professionalism and dedication to his clients and the community. This allowed me to learn from not only a prime example – but the prime example of a professional.

These giants have laid the groundwork for my journey as a young professional, and they have been guiding figures in how I strive to continually learn to lead. From here, I hope to be the proverbial shoulders, sharing my own experiences in the form of a handbook, research, and personal stories, on which you may see further.

Table of Contents

Chapter 1: Introduction

Before the YP, there was the Yuppie

In 1984 authors Marissa Piesman and Marilee Hartley released a tongue-in-cheek literary work called the *"Yuppie Handbook."* The one-hundred-plus page guidebook reads more about being pretentious in 1980 than how to be a true professional. Yuppie, coined by the authors, or YUP, stands for Young Urban Professional and can be adapted across a diverse conglomerate: BUPPIE – Black Urban Professional, HUPPIE – Hispanic Urban Professional, and GUPPIE – Gay Urban Professionals. The 1980s satire has not aged well in terms of political correctness and sensitivity to modern readers, but there are similar parallels between the view of young professionals in the 1980s and how that same generation categorizes young professionals of today.[1]

For instance, the Yuppie way is entirely materialistic and obsessed with the finest brand-name accouterments and expensive cuisine. Millennials are viewed as being materialistic in having the finest smart devices, and their avocado spread on rye accompanied by gourmet coffee. However, when reading the *"Yuppie Handbook,"* it is hard not to recognize the great disparities between the two generations. The Yuppie generation was focused on the two-car garage, four-bedroom home in the suburbs or the penthouse loft apartment, two children, housekeeper, nanny, luxury vehicles, and residing on Wall Street in the C-suite. When compared to the YP, generations of today focus on finding employment, not in line with their degree, earning a wage below the poverty line, living at home with their parents, and trying to pay down student loans instead of saving up for the weekend date night.

Paul Taylor in *"The Next America: Boomers, Millennials, and the Looming Generational Showdown,"* defines the two categories of YUPPIES and YPs as follows:

> ***Baby Boomers*** *(born from 1946 to 1964). As exuberant youths led the countercultural upheavals of the 1960s. But the iconic image of that era – long-haired hippie protesters – describes*

---

[1] Piesman & Hartley, 1985.

only a portion of the cohort. Now on the front stoop of old age, Boomers are gloomy about their lives, worried about retirement, and wondering why they aren't young anymore. Icons: Bill and Hillary Clinton, George W. Bush, Barack Obama, Steve Jobs, Tom Hanks. [2]

***The Millennials** (born after 1980). Empowered by digital technology; coddled by parents; respectful of elders; slow to adulthood; conflict-averse; at ease with racial, ethnic, and sexual diversity; confident in their economic futures despite coming of age in bad times. Icons: Mark Zuckerberg, Lena Dunham, LeBron James, Carrie Underwood, Jennifer Lawrence, Lady Gaga.* [3]

The world of the young professional has changed, and the employment and career landscape has changed drastically. However, one thing has remained consistent – both generations consist of ambitious professionals hoping to accomplish something of meaning and purpose. Taylor notes the following:

"Views of Business: Millennials' views of business are not substantially different from those of older generations. On a three-question index of attitudes about business power and profits, Millennials' opinions mirror those of Gen Xers and members of the Silent Generation and are slightly less critical of business than are the view of Baby Boomers. Also, Millennials are about as likely as other cohorts to agree that the country's strength is built mostly on the success of American business." [4]

---

[2] Taylor, 2014.
[3] Taylor, 2014.
[4] Taylor, 2014.

Some of the differences were noted in Keith Ferrazzi's book, *"Leading Without Authority"* in which he outlines old work rules versus new work rules. [5]

Old Work Rules:

1. Your team is limited to those that report to you or report to your manager.
2. Professional relationships happen organically over time and develop without purposeful effort.
3. Leadership is something bestowed upon you by the company or organization.
4. To advance your career, you must do what's expected of you according to your job description.
5. To convince your teammates to tackle a project or mission, you must make a passionate and persuasive case for it.
6. Collaboration is a fallback you resort to when you can't get it done yourself.
7. When it came to growing professionally and developing both hard and soft skills – you looked to your manager, performance reviews, and training programs.

New Work Rules:

1. Your team is made up of everyone inside and outside the company important to achieving your project or mission.
2. Professional relationships must be proactively and authentically developed with the people on your teams.
3. Leadership is everyone's responsibility.
4. To advance your career, you should do whatever it takes to create value for your team in your organization.
5. To invite your teammates to join your project or mission, you must first earn permission to lead through serving, sharing, and caring.

---

[5] Ferrazzi & Weyrich, 2020.

6. Collaboration and partnership with your team members are the new norm and essential.
7. We seek out our team for development and growth; we offer teammates candid feedback needed to develop their skills, performance, and behavior because we are committed to their success and the success of the greater mission.

Young Professional, A Definition

As we begin our journey, we must define the term "Young Professional." What is your own definition of a young professional? Breaking the title into individual parts, young clearly refers to someone in their early years – someone who simply has not had the benefit of time and experience on their side. In defining "professional," I would like to reframe the definition. As I graduated high school, my angsty teenage persona complained to my business teacher that I did not see the point of going to college and earning a degree – she simply stated that a degree would mean the difference between a job and a career. This handbook is not for those simply looking for a job but seeking employment or a career that one can turn into a profession.

The opening chapters of Todd Rose and Ogi Ogas' "*Dark Horse: Achieving Success through the Pursuit of Fulfillment*" argue that following the industrial revolution, employment became increasingly standardized: largely, men were made to fit into systems instead of fitting the systems to men. My interpretation of this metaphor translates into the concept that a machine, or system, can do a job – it is us that can be the profession. In a technological world where machines and computers operate autonomously, the human component finds meaning in their occupation and shapes their profession.[6]

Rose and Ogi recite a study from 2018 in which the think tank Populace surveyed 3,000 men and women and asked, "what constitutes the societal

---

[6] Rose & Ogas, 2020.

view of success and what do they view personally as success?" Of all the respondents, a resounding 91% said that their idea of a successful person was "someone who is purpose-driven." [7]

Therefore, moving forward, let us use the definition of a Young Professional as "someone who is entering the initial stages of their purpose-driven occupation and sculpting a successful profession."

The Young Professional's Handbook, An Overview

The *Young Professional's Handbook's* concept is to provide a clear path from being a young professional to being retired. The *Handbook* reviews the evolutionary paths of humans and their relationship with work as a means of expending or reserving energy from the earliest known human-like beings to the digital world we occupy. Building on our knowledge of the history of work, projections, and hypotheses about the future landscape of professions follow. Misconceptions about current workplace norms and defining characteristics of an individual's career phases will start the reader with a basic understanding of why we work, why we are compelled to work, how work will continue to evolve, and where we fit into the workforce.

By having a basic understanding of the opportunities for a career and knowing the current phase occupied, readers will be able to draft their first employment application materials to include portfolios, resumes, and cover letters. Steps to successfully construct these materials will be outlined in the coming pages for the emerging professional. Candidates are then walked through a detailed process for crafting narratives and interview materials to engage potential employers. Should you receive a job offer, we will also discuss how to negotiate offers along with accepting and rejecting these offers professionally.

---

[7] Rose & Ogas, 2020.

Types of conversations and considerations that will arise during the first years on the job include topics such as networking, asking for a raise or promotion, and seeking out employee development opportunities. Effectively communicating during these conversations and in everyday interactions will assist in your career development. Readers should aim to be indispensable employees within the workplace as valued and respected individuals.

Young Professionals in Perspective

One of the best career-finding advice narratives can be found in Richard N. Bolles' *"What Color is Your Parachute 2020,"* a publication that is updated yearly and contains information on seeking employment. Within the introductory chapters, Mr. Bolles notes some remarkably interesting statistics that outline the job market that Young Professionals face following the Great Recession (it is noteworthy that the 2020 version is quoted here, and the outlook may drastically change due to the 2020-2021 pandemic). Between the years 1994 and 2008, roughly half of all active job seekers found a job or employment within their first five months of searching; during the same time frame, roughly 10% of job seekers took a year or longer to find gainful employment. However, in the years following, those taking a year or longer to find employment jumped to 17%-30%, followed by an estimated 20.8% taking six months to a year, 13.9% finding employment within three to six months, and only 30.1% were able to find a job within one to three months. Shockingly enough, for those aged between 18-24 years old, an estimated 69% had jobs that lasted a year or less and were back to job searching. For those aged 35-44 years, the estimates did not improve much, with only 36% having a job for the same period. Even then, of those in the older age group, an astounding 75% had a job that lasted five years or less. Bolles also notes that Baby Boomers born between 1957 and 1964 held an average of 11.9 jobs between the ages of 18 to 50. The initial statistics show how difficult the hiring landscape was following the Great Recession and prior to the COVID-19 pandemic. However, the second set of statistics dispel any stereotype that Millennials, Gen-Z, and Gen-X continually job-hop from one employer to the other as a new paradigm where their parents' generation did the same.

Section Summary

The idea of a Young Professional is not a new concept and dates back over forty years. The idealistic futures that Young Professionals aspire toward has changed. No longer are generations seeking name brand merchandise or the "American Dream," but instead hope to find some semblance of financial security, make a difference in the world they occupy by fulfilling a purpose larger than themselves, and working collectively for the betterment of their peers and generations to come. Young Professionals will no longer be limited to white-collar individuals with bachelor's or master's degrees but will cover a diverse conglomerate of individuals working in new professions. YPs will be purpose-driven to accomplish something of meaning.

This handbook will outline aspects such as figuring out why work has evolved from its earliest inception to the modern era. Career phases are strategically described, and the aspects of attaining each will be provided. Basic applicant materials such as resumes, and portfolios are detailed; opportunities for networking to help find new positions allow Young Professionals to get these resumes and portfolios into the hiring manager's hands even faster. After the materials have been distributed and networking undertaken, interviews will abound, and this handbook will walk applicants through the process of achieving a successful interview. Effective communication and ways of finding healthy organizations to foster employee development are described to allow you the opportunity to evaluate future employers, understand the ins and outs of your current place of employment, or be translated into the factors that today's workforce is seeking. Other aspects such as timing your career and planning for your retirement round out the topics discussed to bring the full scope of a person's career into perspective – from start to finish, resume to retirement.

Chapter 2: Professions: Then, Now, and the Future

Skilled at Developing Skills: Human Evolution and the Energy of Work

Author James Suzman in his work "*Work: A Deep History from the Stone Age to the Age of Robots*," notes that the only commonly held definition of work throughout the evolution of humans reads as such: "*work is the act of purposely expending energy or effort on a task to achieve a goal or end.*" Suzman continues that work has always been a transaction of energy, and the capacity creates the difference between living and dead organisms. "*Work*" brings to light the evolution and cultural journey that has created the world we currently occupy. [8]

When animals began utilizing tools to access food and superiority over other animals, a surplus or abundance of resources allowed for these same animals to focus their attention elsewhere. This excess energy allowed time to craft more and more tools without losing or expelling once precious resources. Generating additional resources and tools led to the first skilled craftsmen. Thus, Suzman speculates that humans became skilled at developing skills. [9]

Humans are by nature social animals and as we evolved, mimicked skills being crafted and harnessed by other humans we observed within our societies or tribes. During this point in our evolution, we slowed in the progression of innovating new skillsets due to the attempt to catch up to one another in our abilities. Once the common set of skills are adopted within the social unit, social learning was then transmitted across generations. This social learning allowed humans to start further in their evolution at a younger age than the generations preceding them.

At some point within our evolution, the reserve energy of our species increased significantly with the harnessing use of fire. The nutritional value found within our foods increased, and the strength of our tools increased as we began molting ores into iron. The greater the surplus of

---

[8] Suzman, 2021.
[9] Suzman, 2021.

energy and effectiveness of our tools allowed for more time for other activities such as reproduction of new skills, new methods of crop cultivation, and even reproduction of our species. The abundance of resources and reproduction of humans grew in balance opening the world to a new sphere of opportunities and trades as larger villages turned to towns and eventually to cities and metropolises. [10]

Working Class: A Class on Working

As our towns and cities began to grow, new trades and occupations rose to accommodate the necessities of everyday life. These new areas of work then broke into divisions of labor in which French Sociologist Emile Durkheim wrote about his groundbreaking dissertation *"Divisions of Labor in Society"* in 1893. Within the introduction of the 1984 edition, German American sociologist Lewis A. Coser provides an insight discovered within Durkheim's work. Following what Durkheim considered the basic differences between modern and simple societies (as such in 1893), Coser notes the sociologist turned his attention to legal codes. Interestingly, Durkheim found that two types of legal regulations ruled two different societies. He continues,

> *"He asserted that legal regulations, that is, rules of conduct that are sanctioned, can be roughly divided into two major types: repressive sanctions, which are characteristic of penal law and involve punishment for transgressions and deviance; and restitutive sanctions, which, in contrast do not rely on punishment but rather rely on righting of a balance upset by the violation."[11]*

> *"The predominance of penal or restitutive law in given societies, Durkheim argued, could serve as an index of the type of society, or the type of solidarity under consideration.*

---

[10] Suzman, 2021.
[11] Durkeim, 2014.

Societies based on mechanical solidarity relied almost exclusively on penal sanctions. What was punished was a departure from the collective way of life, the shared values, and beliefs of the society. Any action that was perceived as an infringement of the collective consciousness – the shared mental and moral orientations of societies – was conceived as a crime and sanctioned accordingly. In modern societies, on the other hand, in which individuality, and hence the violation of individual rights, is central, restitutive rather than penal sanctions predominate."[12]

Let us then consider a few of the defining points in time where a significant change occurred while comparing their impact, as Durkheim has noted, being societal solidarity. The Stone Age consisted of humans learning from one another the ability to utilize stone tools and generate the abundance of energy resources, as noted within the *Skilled at Developing Skills* section. Once the majority mastered the use of these tools, they became machines within the production of resources and created a sense of the "collective consciousness" for the human race – everyone used these same tools to create housing and shelter. Those not developed enough, or resistive to change, would steal food or shelter from others. This would cause an infringement of the societal norm, and the offender would be considered a criminal and punished as such – an eye for an eye, tit-for-tat punishment. We can then postulate that a sense of right and wrong or a protocol for humans to follow emerged for the tribe or village to prosper and evolve. The protocols would allow the skilled beings to become more individualized within their familial or tribal clans. A sense of unfairness inflicted on someone in the unit would be viewed as immoral by the collective consciousness. Thus, a fear of punishment for any unfairness propelled humans to interact congenially with one another and led to a greater stockpile of resources. Humans were less likely to infringe on the rights of others and instead contributed to their unit and worked alongside one another.

---

[12] Durkeim, 2014.

As noted in the *Skilled at Developing Skills* heading, excess resources set the stage for harnessing fire and the birth of the Iron Age. Humans began producing more robust tools and housing. Again, the collective unit would learn skills from one another to better their clan and stockpile additional resources. They became a mechanical unit that sustained more and more reserved energy. Those resistive to the advent of iron tool making would revert to stealing or pillaging nearby villages. The emergence of crime revealed another introspective look at the penal sanctions imposed on transgressors. In effect, a new level of normalcy for the individual protection of rights is established.

The Age of Enlightenment or the Reformation was birthed through the invention of mass-produced books calling on individuals to become literate, and the collective literacy rate rose within society. Following this, more divisions within the society grew between the literate and illiterate and created wealth and opportunity gaps. As those afforded the chance to become literate at an early age began to make their mark on society, new inventions rapidly arose. These innovations would lead to the Industrial Revolution, where people again became tools to create more machines. As this form of work or profession evolved, people created their own individual identities and called upon civil rights advocates and labor unions to better working environments. As this same generation began to retire, governments were called upon to provide retirement for their constituents, which resulted in such programs as Entitlements. Now, as we have turned the corner of another century where societies started as machines, evolved to individuals through penal regulation, the Millennial generation is afforded the opportunity to exercise more restitutive regulations.

The Entitled Generation Views of an 'Entitled Generation'

Unfortunately, as the Millennial, Gen-X, and Gen-Z cohorts begin implementing the restitutive regulations deemed necessary for the moral treatment of humans instead of penal violations of treating them as part of a machine, they have somehow been received as the "Entitled Generation." However, as we have seen thus far, this desire to be seen as a human individual and not as the proverbial cog-in-the-wheel is merely a part of our own evolution as new tools and technologies emerge, mature, and stagnate.

A Trial in Family Assistance Programs

Author James Livingston writes in his book "*No More Work: Why Full Employment is a Bad Idea*," of the employable adults in the United States, 25% are paid less than the official poverty line meaning that 1 in 4 children living in the United States grows up in poverty. More astounding is the statistic that nearly one-half of all American adults are eligible for food stamps.[13] Livingston also posits that two-thirds of all non-cognitive task jobs will be eliminated in the next twenty years, a statistic he obtained from a 2012 book: "*The Race Against the Machine*." [14] Since 1959, the fastest-growing component of household income – prior to the 2020-2021 pandemic – has been some form of government transfer payments. At the turn of the millennium, 20% of all household income came from this form of payment through welfare or entitlements. If this number seems staggering, without the same programs, half of all adults capable of working full-time would have lived below the poverty line, and most working US citizens would have qualified for food stamps. From 1920-2020, Livingston notes that economic growth has occurred while private investment has not, meaning that profits, in his opinion, are pointless and only signifies that business is thriving while employees are not. [15]

In April 1970, the House of Representatives in the United States voted for the Family Assistance Plan, FAP, to guarantee an annual income for all households in need. Studies of this program revealed that those

---

[13] Livingston, 2016.
[14] Livingston, 2016.
[15] Livingston, 2016.

receiving payments without working barely changed their work ethic. However, the work ethic of those who received payments while working increased relative to those not receiving payments. As a result, men reduced their work week by one hour while women reduced their average work week by five hours. Women tended to spend more time with family by helping children do homework, picking children up from daycare, and other familial responsibilities typical of a family in 1970. Women within the study chose more "free" time as the average household wealth increased and spent this time with their children. However, as Livingston notes, the exact inverse has occurred within the workplace since the 1980s. When comparing the Family Assistance Plan to welfare programs, on average, the cost to implement FAP would cost $72-$96 per family annually, while current estimates of welfare programs cost $200-$300 annually per family. This leads Livingston to ask the question: "how does one make a living without a job?" Ultimately, the Family Assistance Plan was terminated shortly after its enactment, and the American way of life became as we know it today. [16]

The New Economy, The Gig Economy

In looking toward, the future trends of the global workplace, Marion McGovern, author of *"Thriving in the Gig Economy: How to Capitalize and Compete in the New World of Work,"* provides a synopsis of recent trends leaning toward the "gig economy." The commonly held definition of a gig-worker consists of an individual performing a single professional engagement for a short duration. This emerged during the Great Depression as business owners hired day laborers to perform a day's worth of work to provide income for these families in need. She also cites a Rand-Princeton University study that looked at growth among different types of workplaces. The study reveals that during the timeframe from 2005-2015, the traditional workforce didn't expand – at all. However, "alternative forms of work" grew by an astounding 67%.

---

[16] Livingston, 2016.

Powerhouse Gallup provided additional information where only one in three employees in today's workplace feel any sense of engagement, whereas for every 2 out of 3 employees working independently felt fulfillment. The same study noted that of respondents that began working for themselves, 80% said they could never imagine going back to a traditional work setting. [17]

McGovern also notes two types of economies that have emerged within recent decades thanks to different technological advances: the "On-Demand Economy" and "The Sharing Economy." The on-demand economy relies on fast services performed nearly instantaneously, whereas the sharing economy relies on individuals sharing excess resources such as ridesharing, room renting, among many others. With these new emerging ways of doing business, following the Great Recession, a large contingent of the Gen-Xers within the labor pool became independent workers within the gig economy. Polling of these individuals revealed that 47%, nearly half of all respondents, said their prior employer failed to understand their value and was a main deciding factor in becoming gig-workers. [18]

We Trust No One but Listen to Everyone

McGovern relays in her writing that within the marketplace, people no longer trust or put faith in large corporations; however, they rely heavily on feedback from fellow users. Previous generations would remain loyal to a brand or company. Consider the oft-referenced book "*Good to Great: Why Some Companies Make the Leap and Other's Don't*" by Jim Collins, where the author investigates examples of companies that transitioned from good to great. Eleven businesses stood out – Abbott Laboratories, Circuit City Stores, Fannie Mae, Gillette Company,

---

[17] McGovern, 2017.
[18] McGovern, 2017.

Kimberly-Clark, Kroger, Nucor, Philip Morris, Pitney Bowes, Walgreens, and Wells Fargo. [19]

Of the eleven great businesses, some have undergone further scrutiny that reveals suspicious behaviors that, perhaps, show a different view of how the companies became "great." Philip Morris, now Altria Group, Inc. is a leading producer of tobacco – and leading producer of lung cancer and other health issues related to their products. [20] Wells Fargo & Company has had a laundry list of questionable business practices to reach the number one banking position in 2015, only to be fined in 2020 a lofty $3 billion by the United States Department of Justice and the Securities and Exchange Commission for opening additional accounts for existing customers without their knowledge. [21] Fannie Mae used student loan practices to grow their coffers and faced scrutiny for deliberately overcharging the United States Government and effectively resulted in the U.S. lending directly to students rather than outsourcing through private lenders. [22] Circuit City Stores filed for bankruptcy in 2008, only seven years after making Collins' list. [23]

One year prior to the 2001 listing of Nucor on the "*Good to Great*" list, Nucor paid $98 million to the United States Department and the United States Environmental Protection Agency due to their poor record of controlling toxic emissions. [24] In 2008 Kroger was cited by Greenpeace for selling seventeen out of twenty-two "Red List" species of fish – the Red List catalogs threatened or endangered species that are at risk of extinction. [25] Gillette Company underwent an injunction that stated Gillette's advertisements of the "best ever" products mislead consumers; the UK Office of Fair Trading has investigated Procter & Gamble (who acquired Gillette) for price setting. [26] Abbott Laboratories was fined in

---

[19] Wikipedia, Good to Great
[20] Wikipedia, Alteria
[21] Wikipedia, Wells Fargo
[22] Wikipedia, Fannie Mae
[23] Wikipedia, Circuit City
[24] Wikipedia, Nucor
[25] Wikipedia, Kroger
[26] Wikipedia, Gillette

2012 for selling one of its products for uses not approved by the Federal Drug Administration and an additional $198.5 million for illegal marketing of the drug. [27] Of the eleven "great businesses" generations today would not trust, or due to bankruptcy cannot trust, eight of the eleven candidates. Furthermore, these are only eight out of eleven notable businesses and do not include other companies performing similar business tactics to mislead consumers resulting in a greater need for consumers to rely on feedback from their peers through ratings, comments, and reviews. If current generations use their purchasing power based upon reviews instead of brand or corporate loyalty, they will also do so with their career trajectories. This may mean growth in more professions becoming common place within the gig-economy or listening to peers working as current employees at prospective places of employment rather than basing it solely on the company's brand or name.

If You Want to Know What's Going On, Don't Ask the Boss

To assess recent trends within professions and projected areas of growth, the trusted research firm: *Gallup* proves instructive. Findings from their largest study of the future of work, and as noted in their publication "*It's The Manager*," by Jim Clifton and Jim Harter, as of 2019, there were roughly six million businesses in the United States. Of these six million businesses, approximately four million are considered small businesses, meaning they house four employees or less. Of these six million businesses, the bulk of the employees, an overwhelming 85% of respondents, noted that they were disengaged or unsatisfied at their workplace. This statistic only leaves 15% of all United States employees having any sense of engagement. [28]

---

[27] Wikipedia, Abbot Laboratories
[28] Clifton & Harter, 2019.

Gallup recommends that young professionals seek six key factors in selecting a future place of employment to enhance their own level of engagement. These factors include the following:

1. The current workforce does not seek a position based on the paycheck – instead, they work for a purpose. Considerations should be given to how the prospective or current position allows you to pursue a purpose and not simply a paycheck. The purpose then leads to the second key factor,

2. Consider how the place of employment allows you to pursue professional and personal development. Seek out positions that offer employee development within and outside the place of work, along with opportunities that allow you to grow as a person.

3. Thirdly, consider if the position has a boss or a coach. Mentors and coaches provide leadership that far exceeds those merely filling the boss role. Coaching works best when it falls under the fourth factor,

4. Ongoing conversations consist of instantaneously shared responses or feedback.

5. Find a strengths-based work environment. Dwelling on weaknesses proves costly and nonproductive. When seeking a position or evaluating your current role, consider how well the organization helps you develop your strengths – if your initial interview consists of questions regarding your greatest weakness, this may indicate that the company has a weakness-focused mindset rather than asking about strengths and how they can be best utilized to grow the business.

6. The final factor is determining happiness within the profession by asking, "how does this job allow me to better my life?" Within the question itself, consider how the position allows you to make contributions, grow in strengths, and provide opportunities to do what you enjoy every day. [29]

These six key factors will assist you in your first steps at finding a profession. Ferrazzi, in his book *"Leading Without Authority,"* quotes a 2016 Deloitte survey of HR professionals where only 24% of companies with 50,000 employees or more still follow the standard hierarchical model. [30]

> *"Organizations, the report said, 'are shifting their structures from traditional functional models toward inter-connected flexible teams.' The report continued, 'the entire concept of leadership is being radically redefined. The whole notion of positional leadership that people become leaders by virtue of their power or position is being challenged. Leaders are instead being asked to inspire team loyalty through the expertise, vision, and judgement.'"* [31]

During my high school years, I worked for a grain elevator with several other men – one of which was a particularly quick-witted, gray-haired gentleman named Jerry. One sunny afternoon, we all congregated in the office discussing some of the work we had performed earlier that morning. My employer, Shannon (by the way, thank you, Shannon for taking a chance on a quiet 15-year-old kid, those years built a foundation offered nowhere else, and I often think back to how you handled situations and how a "boss" should be), was asked a question about an order by a customer that had just walked in the door. I answered before Shannon had time to turn from his desk, "we finished the order this morning, and we have it ready to go." Jerry, being the quick-witted guy he is, briskly followed up, "Don't you know if you want to know what's

---

[29] Clifton & Harter, 2019.
[30] Ferrazzi & Weyrich, 2020.
[31] Ferrazzi & Weyrich, 2020.

going on, don't ask the boss." In some instances, the manager does not always know the day-to-day activities or concerns of their employees but focusing on Harter and Clifton's six key factors above will allow you the opportunity to find an attentive manager, just like Shannon was for me.

"Nine Lies about Work: A Freethinking Leader's Guide to the Real World," written by Marcus Buckingham and Ashley Goodall, outlines additional key engagement factors that you can use in your evaluation of workplaces. Here are their criteria:

1. I am enthusiastic about the mission of the company.

2. I clearly understand what is expected of me.

3. I am surrounded by people who share my values.

4. I can use my strengths every day at work.

5. My teammates have my back.

6. I know I will be recognized for my excellent work.

7. I have great confidence in my company's future.

8. In my work, I am always challenged to grow.[32]

In both lists, the research reveals that employees seek out certain aspects within their professions. Buckingham and Goodall break these into two specific categories – interactions and experiences. You will be much happier when considering your own experience: clearly knowing what is expected of you, having the opportunity to use your strengths, and being recognized for them, and being challenged to grow. The interaction

---

[32] Buckingham & Goodall, 2019.

category consists of making sure values and mission align with your values and are practiced and observed regularly by the company, having coworkers and coaches who can mentor you and cultivate your strengths, and having confidence in yourself, your coworkers, and your employers.[33]

Interactions vs. Experiences in Teams

Interactions and experiences are often impacted heavily by additional forces. How you react and interact with those around you, absorb feedback, and how your actions can spread to others. Additionally, you must also realize how others same actions impact your growth within the company and cooperation level within teams. Goodall and Buckingham performed a study within 19 different countries that showed virtually all work is teamwork. Their results showed that companies with 150 employees or more indicated that 82% worked on a team and 72% working on more than one team. This does not apply only to large companies. The same research revealed that smaller companies of twenty or fewer employees had similar results – 68% worked on a team, with 49% stating that they worked on two or more teams. [34]

These teams have oversized impacts on businesses. For example, Buckingham and Goodall's study also showed that those who worked on teams had scores on their eight factors of engagement that ranked twice as high as those who did not work on teams. Even more so, those who trusted their team leader were twelve times more likely to be engaged at work. Considering that work has become more and more team-oriented, employees can readily be twice as engaged as earlier generations who worked alone – if we can become trusted within these groups, that level increases again even more. [35]

---

[33] Buckingham & Goodall, 2019.
[34] Buckingham & Goodall, 2019.
[35] Buckingham & Goodall, 2019.

Prestigious Careers

The word "prestige" comes from the Latin word *praestigium*, meaning illusion. Later the word took on a meaning of admiration or respect built upon the basis of perception, i.e., "a prestigious career," which means that it is only the perception of a career. Oftentimes in life, you will hear what makes for a prestigious career – for this, we look to some of the misconceptions or illusions presented to us as we have navigated the workplace. *"Nine Lies about Work: A Freethinking Leader's Guide to the Real World*," written by Marcus Buckingham and Ashley Goodall, outlines a few of these misconceptions that you may have been taught when pursuing a career.

> **Misconception #1:** Everyone cares which company they work for.
>
> *Reality:* From previous points made, the reader may find that current generations work for a purpose, seek out strengths-based work environments that offer growth opportunities. Echoing these concepts in his book *"The Millennial Whisperer*," Chris Tuff cites a Deloitte Millennial Survey in which 86% of respondents believed that a company's success and mission should be more than just financial performance. Taking it a step further, 65% of those same respondents said that companies should benefit society in some way. When looking for potential places of employment, consider how their values and mission align with your views; Tuff cleverly states that Millennials should choose personality over pedigree – while the brand or company may seem appealing, evaluate its mission and values to find alignment with your own. [36]

---

[36] Buckingham & Goodall, 2019.

Misconception #2: The best plan wins.

Reality: The reality is that the best plan does not always win. The more intelligent plan succeeds. Gather information to base your resolutions upon – Tuff even notes that in the modern world, generations have been able to obtain instant feedback (i.e., text messages, instant messaging apps, push notifications on emails, etc.) – which is helpful for teams. This instantaneous feedback is what Buckingham and Goodall define as a quick "Check-In" that should happen frequently. The instant and frequent feedback may not always be quality feedback, but the repetitiveness and frequency can be beneficial. [37]

Misconception #3: Companies cascade goals.

Reality: To summarize their chapter, companies should not set out to set goals; that is your, as the employee, job, and your job alone. Goals set voluntarily are more likely to be accomplished and provides more benefit for you. The firm or company should focus on meaning and allow you to set the goals. A friend that I have the pleasure of knowing through our volunteering together with a regional young professional's organization offered to peer review an early draft of this writing. As a Human Resource professional, she noted in her feedback that she agreed that employees should take ownership of their goals, and it is their responsibility to align those goals with the company's mission and values. [38]

---

[37] Buckingham & Goodall, 2019.
[38] Buckingham & Goodall, 2019.

Misconception #4: The best people are well-rounded.

Reality: The best employees are probably not the most well-rounded. Think of areas where you excel and go from there; if you are in a managerial position, Goodall, and Buckingham note "adjustable seats" in which one method for increasing productivity from one team member may not illicit the same results from others – tailor leadership techniques to the individual. [39]

Misconception #5: People need feedback.

Reality: Buckingham and Goodall's research reports that it is not necessarily feedback that we, you, and I often seek or need most. What we truly need is attention – uncritical attention at that. Knowing that someone at your place of work sees you, hears you, and focuses their attention on you boosts morale immensely. Furthermore, the authors propose that focusing feedback – or attention – on weaknesses to improve upon is inefficient. Managers should focus praise on strengths so that candidates can capitalize on what is already working to foster more productivity. [40]

Misconception #6: People can reliably rate other people.

Reality: Personally, this is one of my favorite misconceptions. As a young kid, I would watch – repeatedly – the Burt Reynolds movie: "*Smokey and the Bandit.*" One key piece of dialogue has Burt Reynolds' character, the Bandit, conversing with Frog, Bandit's pet name for Sally Field's character, "How stupid you

---

[39] Buckingham & Goodall, 2019.
[40] Buckingham & Goodall, 2019.

are depends on which part of the country you're standing in." [41] I always got a chuckle from that line. Rating systems, however, implemented, cannot be measured in equal or consistent terms. Each system and evaluator have a different understanding of the parameters. As human beings, we cannot rate one another on their competencies or abilities, but instead, the only thing we can truly rate is our own personal experience. [42] Instead of rating abilities, we should be inquisitive and learn about their perspective and personal experiences. For instance, here is another story from my high school years.

In seventh grade, teenage boys were being teenage boys – obnoxious and loud. The girls were giggling and flipping their hair, trying to get the attention of obnoxious boys. A teacher at her wit's end, frazzled and about to lose her, and my apologies for the technical term – but she was about to lose her shit. She was a middle-aged woman, her own children grown and moving on to their own new lives with college degrees, spouses, and children of their own. She is the image of caring. Not only was she a teacher but also a coach – not your typical coach at that. She was the life coach at practices, stern and fixated where needed, caring, and encouraging when getting others to come out of their shells, and never speaking ill of anyone. I usually sat somewhere in the middle of the classroom; as an introvert, I didn't like the spotlight – I aimed just to blend in. Not popular. Not awkward, or at least not too much, I hope. I was middle of the row, quiet and meager most of the time. While waiting for the class to start, my classmates are darting and farting around as teenage boys do, and the girls pass notes and gossip.

"Garric, I need to see you in the hall."

What? What did I do? I was sitting there sketching in my notebook, waiting to learn – or endure – who knows what. I

---

[41] Smokey and the Bandit, 1977.
[42] Buckingham & Goodall, 2019.

don't think I was ever called to the principal's office. I was usually sent down to my mother's classroom. It is incredibly difficult to pull any stunts in a small school where your mother shares the lunch table with some of your teachers.

I walk outside, the teacher trailing behind me. She closes the door and puts a hand on the concrete block wall painted with that latex, off-white paint that comes standard in all schools. She leans on the hand on the wall, bows her head, and shakes it in disapproval.

"Garric, what am I going to do with these idiots?"

Hold on. Did you? Did I hear? Wait…

"I just cannot get them under control, they won't behave, and they're bouncing all over the place in there. What do I need to do to get through to them?"

At that point, her voice was breaking, a little defeated exasperation cracking at the end. We were students; we never really thought about how our teachers felt. We merely endured the day until we were released for whatever practice for whatever sport. How many more months until summer break?

I was shocked when she uttered these words. I knew that she did not mean to call them idiots. She had just reached the point of exhaustion, and in her defense, my classmates could be a bit relentless. I stood there with her as she hung her head with her eyes closed. She cared. You could just feel it, and this was killing me that I had nothing I could do to help. I wasn't a teacher's pet, but I also wasn't the class jackass. To this day, I have no idea what I said in response. I was still shocked that a teacher, an adult, was reaching out to me with this mildly inappropriate question – but it was because she cared. I wish I could remember what I said. It wasn't wise or prophetic in any manner – obviously if I cannot even remember. Whatever I may have relayed to her was ultimately incorrect. I was 14; how could I know?

Not until years later would I understand the answer I should have given her. I was reading a book by one of my favorite authors, Adam Grant. In his book "*Give & Take*," he describes her situation as compassion fatigue, or better known as being burnt out. All your hard work seems to be given without making an impact. He also describes a study in which those who grew up to have 'talent' or were 'diamonds in the rough' generally became that way as a self-fulfilling prophecy. Somewhere in their life, someone believed in them and provided them the care and attention they needed to excel. A Harvard study revealed as much when teachers would spend extra time coaching and mentoring students who they were told they would have the capability of excelling. Grant continues by telling the narrative of CJ Skender, an accounting professor who has taught over 35,000 students throughout his career and has become a decorated educator. His peers often think that he has the ability to find talent – and he does – only he finds that every student is capable of harnessing talent.

If I were my 14-year-old self, standing with my teacher again now, and she asked that very same question – I would tell her to do the same with each of the students. Pull each one out in the hall individually and ask what they needed from her to reach them. That act in and of itself would have resonated more than anything. I had the white privilege of the education system in that my teachers knew my mother was a teacher and one of their colleagues. I had been tested as one of the "gifted kids" and was found to have an IQ of 129 in the sixth grade – that IQ was low-end 129, I should add. Borderline gifted is what they had termed me. Borderline something, but it sure as hell wasn't gifted. However, these traits, a mother who was a teacher, presumed "giftedness" (whatever that means), led teachers to lean on me and show the added attention. What if we thought all students, all employees, all friends were gifted? Talented. Worthy of the extra attention. How far would that translate, and how much more engaged and empathic would we all be?

When we consider this in terms of ratings versus the experiences – how could we rate my classmates on a cooperative level? No one would have the definitive, clear-cut rating schedule… but instead, what if we had considered the experience had by each individual student and the teacher? This story also relays into the next misconception; read on to see how.

Misconception #7: Everyone has potential.

Reality: My distressed teacher assumed that I had potential; however, everyone has potential – that part is true – what everyone should focus on is how individuals harness this potential through, as Buckingham and Goodall note, momentum. [43] Everyone will learn at their own pace, and they have the ability to learn and gain knowledge, skills, or trades – but managers or hiring professionals should look to the concept of momentum and how quickly these skills may be acquired. After roughly six years in my current firm and seeing high turnover, I soon found this technique truly works. Generation Z and Millennials grew up with technology, and future generations will know nothing but technology – I was less concerned about which programs or software the potential candidates currently possessed, so I evaluated them on their ability for momentum. Since then, every employee has been able to harness their own momentum and the firm reached a financial milestone it had not achieved in nearly 40 years in business.

---

[43] Buckingham & Goodall, 2019.

Misconception #8: There is such a thing as work-life balance.

Reality: Instead of attempting to seek ways of separating work from personal life and vice versa. Find life within work – find employment that is fulfilling and allows you to enter a state of flow. [44]

Misconception #9: Leadership is a thing.

Reality: Write down your definition of leadership. The chances are that each reader will have their own definition of leadership. The reasoning behind Buckingham and Goodall's premise is that people only attain leadership if they have followers. Each follower has their own concept of what makes a good leader or who they choose to dedicate their loyalties to. Therefore, leadership may not necessarily be the important factor, but a reflective or introspective follower that knows who they are, what they value, and what traits and characteristics are important to them define who they view as leaders – all of which cannot be quantified into a single form of leadership, simply an individual that they relate to and find commonalities with. [45]

Section Summary

As a commonly held concept, work is the expending of energy to achieve a goal or end. As humans have evolved through time, energy reserves have allowed them to continually develop new skills – and even became skilled at developing skills. Tools, machines, and robots continue the overall reserve of energy, allowing humans to be more resilient and social. Harnessing resources such as fire and tools boosted the nutritional

---

[44] Buckingham & Goodall, 2019.
[45] Buckingham & Goodall, 2019.

value of the food supply, and extra energy was focused on reproduction and innovation. The new areas of innovation created a need for trades and divisions of labor. Trade, bartering, and transactions between this diverse atmosphere of tradesmen, farmers, and merchants contributed to the advent of money. Once all aspects combined, rules and laws have evolved to create a balance between humans and the labor they create. Through the ages, generations experience an imbalance in labor and value and readjust themselves – and the era of the Boomer, Millennial, Gen-X, and Gen-Z may be the adjustment period to allow for a new balance to be struck.

Entitlements, welfare, taxes, and supporting one another lead us all to the necessity of work. However, alternate methods of doing business such as the Gig Economy, The On-Demand Economy, and the Sharing-Economy finds ways of bartering and trading when younger generations have fewer resources to pay in return. It also creates less waste and higher reserves of energy. Distrust in the status-quo, organizational hierarchies, and government programs has led current generations to take control of their careers and direct them in the way they see fit – purposeful and full of meaning. In doing so, Gen-X, Millennials, and Gen-Z have certain aspects they seek in a work environment, mainly with six key factors that can be evaluated against the eight criteria of engagement.

Interactions and experiences will impact workers' engagement levels, and team workplaces are growing in numbers while engagement is dwindling. Current generations are led to follow the path to prestigious careers that only carry the appearance or perception of being a quality career. Misconceptions abound from previous ways of thinking and should be reframed to create a workplace that people would enjoy commuting to daily.

Chapter 3: Career Starters

Defining the Career Phases

Now that we have gained an understanding of the history of work and professions, some of the driving forces for our interest in working, misconceptions, and realities of starting a career, we will now look at the phases of a career as defined by James M. Citrin as he has outlined in his book *"The Career Playbook: Essential Advice for Today's Aspiring Young Professionals."* These phases are:

1. Aspiration Phase

2. Promise Phase

3. Momentum Phase

4. Harvest Phase

5. Encore Phase

6. Legacy Phase

The first phase, the aspiration phase, is a discovery journey of learning, developing skills, and gaining feedback, and typically occurs during college and the first few years into one's career. During the onset of this phase, individuals will make their academic declaration – determining a major, charting the coursework for degrees or certifications, enrolling in post-high school academic settings such as technical schools, community colleges, or secondary education universities. Here, the individual gains the basic working knowledge of a profession or career, notes the desired skillsets needed in a position, and gains credentials. [46]

---

[46] Citrin, 2015.

The second phase, the promise phase, follows graduation, high school, or secondary education and typically endures for about one to seven years into a person's career. This is where Citrin notes that individuals in this phase declare their professional major building on their academic major. The promise phase includes an employer taking a chance on the individual as a potential candidate and offering them a position with their company. [47]

During your early thirties to mid-forties, your experience value will exceed the potential value where the promise noted above begins to pay off for the employer as well as the promise you had given yourself during your academic and promise phases. Individuals will begin to see their accomplishments and build momentum that carries them into their final three phases: harvest, encore, and legacy. [48]

Personalities in the Workplace

As many will come to learn through their careers, personalities can flourish and founder in certain environments. We can see some of these impacts that personalities of teams have on their success rates; however, to know in which environment our personality type will flourish, you must learn which personality type you have and gain an understanding of how you work, who you work best with, and how you hope to grow. A fascinating online tool can be utilized to evaluate your own personality type: 16personalities.com. The website provides everything from personality type definition, dating and relationship advice, strengths and weaknesses, friendships, and career insights. To save time, here are a few key notes about each of the sixteen personalities:

(Readers should note that this is based upon the Meyers Briggs test, which some may not view as the most reputable or trustworthy classification of testing – therefore, they should utilize whichever scale they deem appropriate to them. However, I have been enrolled in various leadership classes and performing the test within our firm. So far, it seems to be fairly accurate, if not mildly unnerving at how accurate the respondents say it is).

---

[47] Citrin, 2015.
[48] Citrin, 2015.

Analysts – INTJ, INTP, ENTJ, ENTP

Architects (INTJ): Career paths best suited for INTJ personality types consist of positions in which they can search out meaningful challenges and finding solutions to important problems. You will want the freedom to share your greatest strengths. You also can condense complex concepts into clear, concise, and actionable paths. Seek out opportunities that show value in allowing you to expand your knowledge and thinking. Try to remember that a dislike of authority without having earned your respect may be problematic – diplomatic communication can help you achieve status with your peers and employers. You will want to seek positions where you can work independently or in smaller groups to improve your own progress and evolution.

Potential Career Paths: project managers, engineers, strategists, analysts. [49]

Logician (INTP): Career paths best suited for INTP personality types harness creativity, theoretical methods, and an entrepreneurial and innovative spirit. You will want to search out positions that seek candidates who seek out models of underlying principles and concepts, are attentive to detail, and self-driven. Prospective managers should be insightful and open-minded to your constant generation of ideas.

Potential Career Paths: scientist, physics, analysts, mathematicians. [50]

---

[49] Architect Personality, 16personalities.com
[50] Logician Personality, 16personalities.com

Commander (ENTJ): Your personality type is bold, driven, and respected. You have the vision, intelligence, and determination despite any obstacle. You will want to seek opportunities to generate a vision of the future, creating achievable strategies and precise execution. Remember to be self-aware and not too assertive when attempting to keep others on track. You will seek out opportunities as executers or entrepreneurs where you can slate a course of your own making and put it to work – especially in a structured, orderly manner.

Potential Career Paths: entrepreneur, executive, manager. [51]

Debater (ENTP): Naturally engaged and interested, you will seek out career paths that allow you to develop solutions to novel, interesting, and diverse problems, both technical and intellectual in nature. Find a position that allows you to use your versatile nature instead of positions that contain monotonous, tedious repetition.

Potential Career Paths: lawyers, psychologists, analysts, scientists. [52]

Diplomats – INFJ, INFP, ENFJ, ENFP

Advocate (INFJ): Advocates do not seek status or marital gain – instead, you find more in a profession – something that aligns with your values. Your ability to see yourself fitting in with any position will allow you to be versatile in your career. Even more, you will hope to find meaning, connection, and facilitation. With a strong communicating presence, you will seek a position that allows independence, non-competitive

---

[51] Commander Personality, 16personalities.com
[52] Debater Personality, 16personalities.com

roles, growth, and leadership. You have the ability to bring people together and build a connection to bridge gaps.

Potential Career Paths: counselors, psychologists, teachers, social workers, spiritual leaders. [53]

Mediator (INFP): Mediators hope to seek out a fulfilling position. Finding something you are truly passionate about seems to be more of a calling than a job. Menial tasks at work will seem frustrating instead of meeting your expectations in which you seek creative outlets, independence in your work, and a longing for connection. Versatility allows mediators to fit into any position as well as be driven freelancers. Nonprofit or marketing in artful ways would provide great directions. Leading a deep inner life, you can express yourself and the work of others in amazing ways.

Potential Career Paths: writers, composers, choreographers, service careers. [54]

Protagonist (ENFJ): People helpers, facilitators, caretakers, ENFJ personality types are warm, sociable, and often have high emotional intelligence. Seek out positions that allow you to be client-facing or in service to others. You can express yourself in a creatively honest manner which allows you to work well with others but not so much with data, statistics, systems, or spreadsheets. Remember to practice self-care – your personality is drawn to burn out in the wrong career path. Practice and hone people skills, your intuitive nature, and diplomatic bridge-building to generate a fulfilling career.

---

[53] Advocate Personality, 16personalities.com
[54] Mediator Personality, 16personalities.com

Potential Career Paths: religious work, teaching, counseling, advising, consulting, human resources. [55]

Campaigner (ENFP): Always drawn to new ideas, ENFP personality types allow themselves to dive deeper into a vast arena of topics versus their counterparts. Campaigners will see a wide array of options for employment from their perspective and can adapt their people skills to network into many career options. The feeling quality of their personality type allows them to harness logic and apply it to human interactions and networks. Seek out positions that allow constant development, shifting approaches, unpredictability, idea exploration, and areas where boundaries can be pushed.

Potential Career Paths: human sciences and services, psychology, counseling, politics, diplomacy. [56]

Sentinels – ISTJ, ISFJ, ESTJ, ESFJ

Logistician (ISTJ): Logisticians will want to seek out stable careers providing long-term growth over time. This personality type will seek dependable working conditions, tradition, respect, authority, security, and consistency. Your preference for working conditions will allow you to work independently with a very defined role. Positions focusing on facts and not feelings will be of great benefit to ISTJs. If the employer is built on the idea of breaking the rules, this position should be avoided at all costs as it will create a tumultuous working relationship.

---

[55] Protagonist Personality, 16personalities.com
[56] Campaigner Personality, 16personalities.com

Potential Career Paths: data analysts, financial managers, administrators, doctors, military officials, judges, lawyers, law enforcement. [57]

Defender (ISFJ): Defenders will fit in best when they are of service to others. They are humble, earnest and remain calm in tense situations. Unlikely to seek the spotlight, ISFJs are uncomfortable in seeking out managerial positions and find security in structured positions. Defenders will want to personalize challenges or situations instead of thinking in abstract ideas. You aim to do good and live a warm, fulfilled life.

Potential Career Paths: medical professions, elementary school teaching, social and religious work, human resources. [58]

Executive (ESTJ): Clear and straightforward are traits executives admire. Organized, structured, and dependable professions appeal most to the ESTJ personality. Your loyalty makes you a perfect fit for organizations seeking long-term staying power from their employees. Striving for ideal representation, executives climb hierarchical ladders well within businesses. You value hard work and a driven self-motivation that you expect to pay off, giving you a sense of great investment in a firm or position.

Potential Career Paths: managerial positions, law enforcement, military, legal firms. [59]

---

[57] Logistician Personality, 16personalities.com
[58] Defender Personality, 16personalities.com
[59] Executive Personality, 16personalities.com

Consul (ESFJ): You are a well-organized individual that brings order and structure to any workplace. Consuls will be happy to work in environments to follow clear and predictable tasks that provide a steady routine. Cooperation among others and positions with interacting with others are among top priorities for the Consul personality type. You will want to seek a position that provides regular appreciation and a sense of helping others.

Potential Career Paths: medical care, social work, administrators, personal accountant. [60]

Explorers – ISTP, ISFP, ESTP, ESFP

Virtuoso (ISTP): One of the most diverse and unpredictable personality types, ISTPs also represent a versatile candidate for employment. They are rooted in a focus on problem-solving, fact-finding, and how things operate. Abstract thinking does not appeal to your personality, and you favor practical knowledge. Critical situations versus structured environments are better suited to candidates of this nature. Freedom and agency matter to Virtuosos, and they are drawn to troubleshooting that provides results.

Potential Career Paths: front-line positions such as paramedics and firefighters, aviation. [61]

Adventurer (ISFP): Imagination and creative powers reign in the world of adventurers. Brilliant in artistic expression of oneself, ISFP candidates seek out experiments, non-competitive environments that focus on shifting conditions,

---

[60] Consul Personality, 16personalities.com
[61] Virtuoso Personality, 16personalities.com

flexibility, and freedom that often lives in the now. Freelance or consulting work allows Adventurers to have agency over their roles.

Potential Career Paths: consultant, artist, musician, photographer, design. [62]

Entrepreneur (ESTP): Entrepreneurs will want to seek out any career path that focuses on action. Quick on your feet, you can adapt to make decisions in the moment, make friends and connections. High social intelligence, improvisational skills, and boldness make ESTP personality types great in positions requiring a higher risk tolerance. Avoid structured organizations with too many rules and restrictions; impatient, energetic, and curious may be used to describe your personality that translates well into observant roles.

Potential Career Paths: sales, negotiating, marketing, acting, athlete. [63]

Entertainer (ESFP): Reflecting on the mood of others allows Entertainers to excel in any career interacting with others. You can respond with great passion, utilize your own resourcefulness, and read others easily. Find employment that fulfills that need to seek intense emotion. Avoid any position where you will be stagnant for long periods, focusing on fine details of data, or require great focus on inanimate objects – you thrive best when building a human connection.

---

[62] Adventurer Personality, 16personalities.com
[63] Entrepreneur Personality, 16personalities.com

Potential Career Paths: EMT, paramedic, nursing, counseling, social work, personal coaching, customer relations. [64]

Now that you know the different personality types and have determined your own, you will be better equipped to know which positions or styles of work you will excel in. Some of Susan Cain's recommendations for fostering your own personality in her writing *"Quiet Power"* include playing to your strengths, following your passion, finding ways of connecting and listening to different personality types as well as your own, and locating a mentor who exhibits a similar work style that matches your own. For example, in her writing *"Quiet: The Power of Introverts in a World that Can't Stop Talking,"* she notes that in most cases, introverted leaders or managers who guide initiative-taking employees make wonderful assets; extroverted leaders who instruct passive employees will garner better results as well. [65]

Another key insight from Cain's writings regard groupthink in which groups can act as mind-altering influences – peer pressure, groupthink, and opinions of coworkers can lead to a change in your own behavior; therefore, be considerate of finding a workplace that has behavior that aligns with behavior you would like to emulate.

Considerations considered thus far – career phases, your own personality, and personalities you interact well with – can all help establish a starting point that you can utilize moving forward. These intangible factors start to influence the business culture, how you will interact with it, shape it, and will be influenced by it.

---

[64] Entertainer Personality, 16personalities.com
[65] Cain, 2013.

Leading from the Bottom

Author Ben Horowitz's *"What You Do is Who You Are"* notes his methods for inclusion in the modern world. He advises his readers to lead from the bottom. This method can be adapted to young professionals starting out, allowing them to take the initiative and find ways of leading – even when first starting a career, or for those who have established their careers – they can adapt the advice to seek out those young leaders to give them opportunities for growth. Horowitz also advises to learn how to negotiate different worlds which can contribute to a broader perspective and help you navigate your career. His three steps are as follows:

1. Involve yourself deeply within the strategy and implementation. Young professionals who can gain a strong understanding of the mechanisms at work and how they are used can quickly become integral parts of the organization. Managers or professionals established in their careers can take note of the very same mechanisms and implementation and seek out young professionals who exhibit strengths that can best fulfill those actions. For example, during the height of the pandemic, a female young professional needed to travel a state away to help care for a family member and their farm. She approached her employer to ask for permission to work remotely from out of state and continue the work being performed at the family farm. Her employer, knowing how important family is to her and keeping the farm running, listened to her needs, and encouraged her to go. Through the process, she set her own schedule and was given deadlines for each of her projects. Her employer has noted her continued great work and commended her drive to deliver her work promptly while maintaining the family farm through her relative's illness.

2. Start with the job description you need to fill. Young professionals may apply to several jobs or positions; however, keep in mind a narrow focus considering your work style, the potential employers' work environment, the different personalities at play, and craft your own job description and seek out those positions that fit your description. On the other hand, professionals seeking out talent for hire, be specific in the job description – future employees will use that description as a baseline for what to expect and know their role from the very beginning. A friend from my college years, we will call her Madison, applied at a local clothing manufacturer as an apparel designer – a position she was excited about because she could utilize her bachelors in Apparel and Textile Design. However, following the first week on the job, the company had only had her working in the call center taking orders and working through customer complaints. This was not the position she was hoping to fulfill and a false advertisement of the role she thought she was filling.

3. Treat people not equally but as family. When we are treated like family, everyone will feel comfortable, safe, and secure. These familial feelings tend to grow loyalty to the organization. For young professionals, building that loyalty with a future employer will allow them to see a candidate that they feel stronger in supporting and mentoring; for established professionals, that sense of belonging will provide a safe environment in which new hires will feel comfortable asking questions and seeking advice. [66]

---

[66] Horowitz, 2019.

Section Summary

Before you begin your career or change careers, having a basic understanding of the career phases allows one to take stock and be introspective of where you are, where you need to go, and what you would like to leave behind. This introspective look will also reveal your own personality, your language of appreciation, and how you might like to operate in the workplace. Often, you will begin your career at the bottom – when transferring careers, you may begin at the bottom yet again. However, strategically understanding how your actions and work ethic can become integral to the work environment will allow you to succeed and find the position that best suits you.

Chapter 4: Career Builders & Accelerators

Defining Ourselves

A man sits at the Saturday morning breakfast table, sipping his coffee and reading the newspaper. His young son rushes in and begins tugging on his arm, shouting, "Dad, let's play, let's play!" Having worked a long week, the man simply just wants a moment to himself to relax, enjoy his coffee, and read the paper. To busy his son for a few moments longer, he pulls out a portion of the newspaper with an intricate, full-page spread of the earth. He proceeds to tear the page into several tiny pieces and tells his son that they will play once he has put the entire picture back together. Dashing over to the kitchen drawer where the roll of tape is kept, the little boy reaches in and races back to the scattered pieces on the kitchen floor. The father contently leans back in his chair again, happy to have a few more moments to himself to enjoy his paper and coffee.

"Done!" shouts the little boy.

"What?!" the father exclaims, thinking there is no way the knee-high little human could have finished putting the map back together so quickly – it probably isn't even right! He leans down and looks at the tattered paper all taped together again with the perfect image of the earth; intricate details perfectly aligned. Dumbfounded, the father asks his son how he managed to get the entire thing back together so quickly.

"It was easy! As I started to put the map back together, I noticed that on the back was part of a man's face! Once I had the man put together, the world fell into place!

Warren Berger recites this parable in his book, "*A More Beautiful Question,*" and it has stuck with me since reading it. The story reflects the depth and beauty of all the characters involved: the son, with his determination, grit, and observant personality, conquered the world by putting man back together; the father, perhaps misguided in his attempt for a moment of solace, was reminded by his son about what truly matters in life. Deeper within the context of the story, one can take away that each individual piece of a man can influence the outcome of the world he sees – that is his character, and the father, son, and the reader all begin to question our own motives and insights into the world, our own character, and the impact we have on our mindset.

Defining Others, Discovering a Target Audience.

A resume and portfolio, in essence, are marketing your self-brand. In applying for a new position, consider the company and structure within the company, such as Human Resources, or employees themselves who perform the interview and hiring process. In evaluating, those performing these tasks might be compared to different consumer groups, which will be described in the coming chapters.

In Citrin's *"The Career Playbook,"* key pieces of advice should also be noted at this stage. When considering drafting and editing your portfolio and resume, also take care to include a cover letter. While technology has changed the hiring landscape, consider asking the potential company whether or not they would prefer physical copies be sent to them for review or if the potential employer would like them sent electronically. In doing so, exchanging any form of communication – always remain professional. During phone conversations, be clear, concise, and refrain from using slang or overly technical vernacular; when emailing, be sure to pay attention to your subject lines, keep emails short and to the point – begin the email with the connection that has introduced you, or the reason for writing. While applying for jobs and new careers can be stressful, always remember that while you may have extra time on your hands as you search for a position, the place to which you are applying may be very busy, so if they do not respond immediately, do not take it as a negative sign – they are simply doing their jobs. On the other hand, be as responsive as you can – after all, they are busy, and you need to find ways to fit within their schedules.

Once we determine who will be viewing the applicant documents and how they prefer to receive them, work on targeting the audience. Brendan Kane takes on the social media aspect of attracting exposure in his book, *"One Million Followers: How I Built a Massive Social Following in 30 Days,"* and this information can be adapted to our own approach in targeting an audience.

1. Have a picture in mind of your audience.
   Research companies through their marketing, websites, social media platforms, and referrals. Outlets such as these will have founders, team members, and key players that may include the people who will be interviewing you. This allows you to have a literal and figurative picture of the person in mind prior to applying for the position.

2. What is the age of your target audience?
   Will you be interviewing with someone who appears to be your age, an industry leader, or maybe a founding member?

3. What is your desired marketing goal?
   Ideally, the desired marketing goal will be to obtain an interview with the company.

4. Where is your audience located?
   Will you be interacting with a company located in a different area, region, or country? With more of the workplace moving online, video and telephone interviews are quickly becoming mainstream as well. Consider these factors when appealing to a prospective employer.

5. What interests do your audience have?
   From item number 1, did you discover any commonalities with the place of business? Does the company have similar values that resonated with your own passions?

6. What other information is available?
    Is there anything else that can be gained from researching the company? What trends are you noticing with your own personal marketing in reaching prospective employers? Is one platform or method outperforming the others?

7. Who are your top competitors, and what does their audience look like? [67]
    Are you competing locally or globally? Are there few candidates for the same position? From my own personal history, four of my peers – and I – interviewed for a firm only to be told a month later that the firm had hired a recent graduate and was no longer accepting part-time interns. This took us all by surprise because we were unaware of this "top competitor" that changed the hiring criteria that none of my peers or I could offer.

Kane notes that one way he achieved his large social media following was due to sharing his message with "Message Champions," who would spread his message at the highest velocity possible. For instance, one of the young professional's organizations that I have most recently worked with launched a social media campaign that showcased one Board member per week. I was able to see the analytics following each Board member's posting. On average, each board member would receive 300-500 views across the platforms; however, one member surpassed the 2,000-view mark – she was a super-connector. Her role within the social media environment outweighed several of our peers, and any time she shared a post, it garnered thousands of views and spread our message much farther than we had anticipated.

---

[67] Kane, 2018.

Turn to another publication that specializes in creating inspiring narratives on a global stage: *"Ted Talks: The Official TED Guide to Public Speaking."* In it, authors Chris Anderson, Tom Rielly, and Kelly Stoetzel outline a toolkit you can use to craft your own life story to be told through your cover letter, resume, portfolio, and interview. As the authors state: your personal narrative should be something that gives more than it takes. Here are the steps to give more to your prospective audience. [68]

Step 1: The initial step in this process is idea building. The authors note that everyone has a story to tell and that our lives are made up of unique events contributing to our own unique life – we must simply craft a journey that everyone can go on together. The authors note the four types of narratives to avoid prior to crafting any of your own ideas: the sales pitch, the ramble, the org-bore, and the inspiration performance. The sales pitch acts to sell, sell, sell. The goal is not to sell yourself as a product but instead to sell your skills as a benefit to the company. How will the employer benefit from hiring you? What will they receive in return for taking a gamble on you? The ramble occurs when the speaker finds themselves in a position where they are nervous and find comfort in trying to explain themselves more and more. Employers will have busy schedules and listening to an hour-long monologue about yourself will agitate them. The creative term, org-bore, refers to the concept that organizations only resonate with those who are already part of them – keep responses about these organizations brief, but on the other hand, if the interviewer is a fellow member of the organization, it could help create a sense of camaraderie. For instance, in college, a classmate approached a founding member of an architectural firm and asked if the gentleman was an alumni member of one of the local fraternities during his time at college. As it turns out, he was. From there, a thirty-minute conversation ensued, and the act of networking commenced without

---

[68] Anderson, 2016.

laboring over how to start the conversation. The final type of narrative to avoid is attempting to be inspirational; the information you present should be inspiring on its own and not based upon your performance. People tend to see through the theatrics and will eventually become bored with the narrative. [69]

Step 2: Consider the through-line. The through-line is a concept that pulls all aspects of your narrative together. Once you have your idea concepts, steps to avoid, and a through-line to intertwine your narrative, you may finally begin outlining your own self-branding materials. For instance, for this section, here is my through-line. [70]

A. Defining Ourselves
B. Defining Others, Discovering a Target Audience
C. Defining Our Journey

I use the outline of first defining and knowing ourselves so that the reader may understand who they will be appealing to and how best to appeal to the audience. The critical concept throughout is "defining;" only once a common definition is developed for each piece can the reader understand the "who, what, how" model. Any applicant can draft a resume and email it to every company on their wish list; however, the approach will provide scattered results and inefficient ways of communicating the applicant's attributes in a way that will reach and resonate with the employer. Here are a few other concepts that authors Anderson, Reilly, and Stotezl say contribute to a compelling narrative:

- Connection – attempt to create or find a connection with your prospective audience, much like my classmate had done in the previous paragraphs. This opens several doors in an effortless way and immediately creates a bond or trust between the two parties. [71]

---

[69] Anderson, 2016.
[70] Anderson, 2016.
[71] Anderson, 2016.

- Narration – create a character the audience can empathize with (in this case, the character will be you and your personal experiences leading to this point in your career); build tension and offer the right level of detail to be effective without rambling and end on a satisfying resolution (accomplishments, achievements, degrees, concepts learned, etc.). To see this in action, the "Acknowledgement" section of this book is my narrative of why I chose to write this book and what I hope to offer you – the reader – in return. My goal is not to sell you my ideas but merely to compile several helpful resources for your benefit, as I have seen these same scenarios unfold through countless other individuals navigating the employment landscape. The stories told within these pages attempt to connect the writings with real-world encounters to help explain the reasoning behind their inclusion in this book. The satisfying resolution for the reader would be to obtain meaningful employment, and my own satisfying resolution would see the timeline for this occurrence to shorten drastically and begin building healthy working conditions as soon as possible. [72]

- Explanation – start where your audience is (are you interviewing with someone who is at a similar position or someone higher in management?), create curiosity or a knowledge gap, bring concepts in one by one using metaphors or examples to create familiarity; and finally create an understanding of the explanation. I hope that this method is shown throughout the book and especially within the previous paragraph.

- Persuasion – reason can change minds forever by breaking down an existing idea or concept, explain why the idea is broken, then lead the audience on a step-by-step journey to a new conclusion. [73]

---

[72] Anderson, 2016.
[73] Anderson, 2016.

Scripting Your Narrative

Anderson, Rielly, and Stoetzel note the importance of scripting: writing out your materials to speak clearly in the moment. This scripting can then be reviewed by peers or mentors for feedback. This feedback can be gained through mock interviews. If you are struggling to craft your personal narrative or defining a personal brand, Kathy Caprino, author of "*The Most Powerful You: 7 Bravery-Boosting Paths to Career Bliss*," note three key questions to ask yourself:

1. How are you special, and how do you stand out in the world?

2. What do you dislike doing?

3. What do you love doing?

Diving even deeper, here are her recommendations for what she references as an internal exploration:

1. What have been your ten greatest accomplishments?

2. What about your personal history has given you a unique perspective?

3. Think about yourself at a younger age – what did you enjoy doing?

4. What comes easily or naturally to you?

5. Consider praise from teachers, friends, colleagues – what was the praise referring to?

6. What negative or positive life events have shaped your life?

7. What are your values?

8. What are the areas you have received special training or experience? What about special praise?

9. What do you enjoy or love being?

10. Where have you made the biggest difference in someone's life?[74]

Caprino also explains the possible four core reasons that people, particularly women, cannot see how important they truly are; reframe these reasons as perceptions to overcome in applying for a position, promotion, or negotiating a career path. Here are her four reasons:

1. People tend to believe that tasks or responsibilities that come easily to them seem unremarkable.

2. The jobs that people have gone badly have left them with a skewed perception.

3. People have not found a job or employment they are passionate about or enjoy and think they are to blame.

4. Employees are encouraged to believe they somehow were not remarkable. [75]

Caprino goes on to explain ways to combat these negative thoughts:

1. *You and People*: Determine who you are and with whom you work well. Keep an eye out for these coworkers when

---

[74] Caprino, 2020.
[75] Caprino, 2020.

interviewing for a new position, as this will reflect who you will work best with.

2. *You and the Workplace*: Contemplate where you have done your best work; whether in solitude or a busy row of cubicles and desks, seek future employment that offers this same type of environment where you already know you can succeed.

3. *You and Skills*: Consider your skill set as opposed to your traits or characteristics. If the first descriptors that come to mind are hardworking, punctual, organized – these are traits and characteristics and not concrete skills. Dig deeper and note the software programs you can use, different equipment you can utilize or operate, subjects you can teach or mentor in. For example, rapidly calculating numbers helps in an accounting capacity, or knowing a camera inside and out may help in marketing, advertising, and photography.

4. *You and Your Purpose in Life*: What are your goals and mission in life? What is important to you outside of work, and can these be integrated into your job search or profession? Having a purpose at work will greatly boost your office morale. My purpose in life was to one day own my own business so that I could have full autonomy over my position. Following graduation, I began working at a firm that had a founder that was seeking a replacement to pass the baton.

5. *You and Your Knowledge*: What do you already know? Have you attended a vocational-technical school and learned a trade? Have you graduated with credentials from secondary education? Do you possess knowledge in niche market areas due to involvement in clubs and organizations?

6. *You and Salary*: Knowing the type of lifestyle that would make you comfortable and most at ease will greatly determine the profession you should try to pursue.

7. *You and Your Geography*: Similar to you and your environment, location and geography play big factors in determining where you will eventually call home or put down roots. [76]

Creating a Resume

I sat down at my desk, ready to begin the day. My employer placed a resume in front of me and said that we had a potential candidate for our office administrator/receptionist position. I began to peruse the contents and noticed a few glaring patterns. The work history seemed somewhat sporadic and short-lived at each of the past employers, but more than that, one single word caught my eye that set the tone for the, again, short-lived experience within our office. The candidate had indicated they worked at a health clinic as a receptionist, and one of the duties was "dealing with doctors and staff." To some, this innocuous phrase might not mean much, but I would implore you to reread the phrase. Professionals should always attempt to show past work history in a complimentary fashion; however, the candidate's use of "dealing" with someone seemed odd. Typically, used terms such as "coordinate with," "work alongside," or "assist" carry positive connotations, whereas "dealing with" carries a tone that implies a complicated relationship between the two parties.

In continuing the theme of consumer groups from previous sections, Marc Cenedella, in his 2019 edition of "*Ladder's Resume Guide*," notes four distinct audiences: screener, recruiter, hiring manager, human resources computer system. [77] Depending on the audience you are

---

[76] Caprino, 2020.
[77] Cenedella, M. (2019). *Ladder's 2019 resume guide* . Ladders, Inc.

addressing will determine, to some extent, how you might craft your resume.

First and foremost, Cenedella notes that applicants must know why they need a resume first: "your resume is a professional advertisement targeted to your future boss with the goal of landing an interview for a job you can succeed in." Cenedella continues to state that the resume is not intended for you – it should resonate with your prospective employer. Once you understand the field you are applying within and the hiring process, you can understand how your resume might be received within their offices. [78]

Cenedella's four audiences, which compared below to Young Me Moon's consumer group types, are simplified here for the purpose of crafting a resume. Moon's consumer group types can be consulted when drafting a resume but might apply best to those in a visual or design field where a portfolio is implemented.

The first audience from "*Ladder's Resume Guide*" is the screener. The screener will likely be someone who sifts through several resumes per day without necessarily being knowledgeable about the field in which you are applying. It's best to use keywords or jargon typical in your field. Likely, they have been given a list of qualities to look for in candidates by their hiring manager, and they will be looking for those who simply check the box next to those attributes. [79]

The second audience consists of the recruiter. Cenedella notes that recruiters will spend, on average, 7.4 seconds viewing your resume before moving on to the next. [80] While this reality may seem intimidating, there are ways of catching the recruiter's eye within that time period to include properly formatting the resume, catchy professional summaries, and making contact with the company before submitting your resume. The third audience, the Hiring Manager, will

---

[78] Cenedella, 2019
[79] Cenedella, 2019
[80] Cenedella, 2019

have a better understanding of the qualities and attributes listed within your resume. [81]

The fourth and final audience is that of an applicant tracking system or computer database that scans your resume for those keywords, much like the screener noted above, but is listed for a different, more practical reason. [82] We list the tracking system, and the database method cannot provide human connection or reasoning when picking or selecting resumes. These systems use artificial intelligence to search for keywords and, as we will see in coming chapters, can be easily confused on the resume file types and layouts.

Now that a common understanding has been established for the reasons behind a resume and who might be viewing the document, an applicant may begin crafting their own resume. *Ladder's* has a simple format to follow when beginning. Start with a blank document, typically within a well-established word-processing software that comes standard or is usually installed on office computers. Refrain from using nonstandard software as formatting and fonts can quickly be lost between the files. [83] (Remember the K.I.S.S. method: keep it simple… students). As a general rule of thumb and commonly accepted as such, keep the format simple, with simple headings and basic fonts, and limit to a single page, although should the candidate have an extensive work history, a second page may be added. *"Ladder's Resume Guide 2019"* notes that format should be kept to a single column, although several examples when searching online reflect a two-column layout. Regarding any recommendations, I would leave this to the discretion of the reader. Attached, I have included my own resume, which can be referenced throughout the reading.

---

[81] Cenedella, 2019
[82] Cenedella, 2019
[83] Cenedella, 2019

Garric Drew Baker, AIA
Bruce McMillan AIA Architects, P.A.
555 Poyntz Avenue, Suite 295
Manhattan, Kansas 66502

Education
Master of Architecture
Kansas State University, 2013

Community Involvement
Manhattan Young Professionals
Advisory Board Committee, 2019-Present (< 1 Year)
Accomplishments:
> Assisted in the planning of the 2018 Kansas YP Summit which brought 300 attendees to Manhattan.

Junction City Young Professionals
Advisory Board Committee, 2014-Present (5 Years)
Accomplishments:
> Longest continuous term of a Board member.
> Assisted in the re-founding the organization.
> Assisted in the planning of the 2019 Kansas YP Summit which brought 150 attendees to Junction City.

Wamego Young Professionals
Advisory Board Committee, 2014-Present (5 Years)
Accomplishments:
> Longest continuous term of a Board member.
> Assisted in the founding of the organization.

Manhattan Arts Center Advisory Board
Advisory Board Committee, 2018-Present (1 Year)
Offices Held: Secretary

Geary County E-Community
Advisory Board Committee, 2015-2017 (2 Year)

AIA Involvement
AIA Central States Region
Advisory Board Committee, 2016-2018 (2 Years)
Accomplishments:
Chaired the University Outreach committee and generated the basis for multiple white papers currently being

AIA Kansas
Advisory Board, 2016-2018 (2 Years)
Offices Held: Associate Director, 2 terms

AIA Flint Hills
Advisory Board, 2018-201 (2 Years)
Offices Held: President-Elect (2019), Secretary (2018)

Historic Preservation Involvement
Kansas Barn Alliance
Advisory Board, 2016-2019 (3 Years)
Offices Held: Secretary (2019), President (2018)

License
Licensed Architect State of Kansas, #7168
License Date: February 2019

Leadership Training
Flint Hills Leadership Class
Alumni, Class of 2014-2015
Accomplishments:
Hosted Earth Day 2015 at Herrington, Kansas which drew 600+ attendees and built ½ mile of trails, planted garden beds, created a community garden, and planted trees with the help of 10+ organizations.

Leadership Manhattan
Alumni, Class of 2017

Professional Awards
Kansas Preservation Alliance
Merit of Excellence, 2019
Woodland Place Stock Farm

Merit of Excellence, 2019
Peace Memorial Auditorium Renovation, Manhattan, KS

Manhattan/Riley County Historic Preservation
Merit of Excellence, 2019
Peace Memorial Auditorium Renovation, Manhattan, KS

KAN-STRUCT 2015
Merit Award, Projects $500,000 or less
Simmons Plaza, Rock Springs 4-H Center

Charitable Works & Volunteering
Wamego Tulip Festival
Volunteer since 2016

Friend of Johnny Kaw, 2017-Present
Donated time and design for the Johnny Kaw Plaza.

Brett Bolton Memorial Plaza, 2012-2013
Donated time and design for the Brett Bolton Memorial Plaza in CiCo Park, Manhattan, KS.

Symphony in the Flint Hills, 2016-2019
Donated time and design for the annual Signature Event.

Hobbies
Outdoor Project Contributor
Contributor of content to the Outdoor Project, an outdoor adventure website; to date, 26 "adventures" have been contributed and 4 articles written covering personal explorations in places ranging from South Dakota to Newfoundland, Canada.

Genealogical Research
Mapping four family trees, one nearly to 1066AD and writing four books to document the family members of each accumulating to nearly 1,000 pages of previously unknown family history.

First in a resume layout would be contact information: name, personal address, phone number, and email address. One item of note is to remember that the screener, recruiter, or hiring manager will be looking at this email address, and it says quite a bit about the applicant. Keep email addresses professional and use up-to-date emailing platforms. [84] (A marketing and media company located here in Manhattan, Kansas, recently launched a rebrand of their company, *middle*. The contact email for the company was "begin@middle.co" ... cleverly, "begin at the middle").

Next is the professional summary. Cenedella asks applicants to keep this portion to a minimum of three or four sentences. Remember, you may only have 7.4 seconds to catch the audience's attention, which is why the professional summary is so important. As noted in Cenedella's writings, the top one-third of your resume should act as a billboard, and the professional summary should be your best advertisement. [85]

The following step for those with professional experience, list the experience in reverse-chronological order with the most recent employment at the top and ending (with no more than ten years shown) with the oldest position held. Keep your dates accurate and titles consistent with positions you held. These attributes can quickly and easily be checked, and nothing sends up a red flag like inaccurate information. [86]

Following previous work experience, is the applicants educational background. Note your highest level of achieved education and list the following in reverse chronological order. [87] *(Please note that the resume I have attached omits the professional summary and puts the education level atop the resume – the resume was submitted for an award with stipulations regarding a degree from an accredited university and licensed within a state under a year. Therefore, these two components*

---

[84] Cenedella, 2019
[85] Cenedella, 2019
[86] Cenedella, 2019
[87] Cenedella, 2019

are front and center for the reviewer). Cenedella notes that the line, "References available on request," is antiquated and not of use in the modern era; however, hiring managers or employers will still likely check references. [88] If the applicant is confident enough to show this item, or list each individual reference, ensure that the individuals will provide positive references that frame your experience well. I have been called upon to provide references in the past and always delight in the opportunity; however, in one instance, the individual and I no longer had a working relationship. A recruiter called and asked for a reference, at which time I had to decline to provide one; sometimes, no referral speaks louder than a poor one. To reframe the conversation, I simply noted that our work relationship was limited to two short months, and I did not have a chance to interact with her often. I clarified that the recruiter should not take my lack of reference in a negative light but that I did not feel it appropriate to provide an adequate reference on a lack of contemporary knowledge. If references cannot be listed or might not provide positive feedback, leave this section off the resume entirely.

The next section of your resume should include a professional summary – a strong caption summarizing the resume, indicating future positions you are pursuing, etc. – and keeping it to a maximum of four lines. Remember, you only have 7.4 seconds to catch the reviewer's attention.

The final section of your resume can include more discretionary items such as achievements, successes, and additional recognitions. These areas, according to Cenedella, should include success verbs: completed, achieved, accomplished, attained, surpassed, etc., etc. He also notes that the more numbers you can reflect in your resume, the better, such as increasing sales by 50%, handling twenty-five multi-million-dollar accounts, etc. This practice shows a specific numerical value that you can bring to the team. [89]

Much discussion has been held on listing social media on resumes – unless your desired field has a social presence or works in a visual field

---

[88] Cenedella, 2019
[89] Cenedella, 2019

such as photography, architecture, etc., do not list social media. Chances are, you have possibly found and reached out to potential employers through online platforms such as LinkedIn, at which time, listing your LinkedIn profile is a waste of valuable real estate on your resume. Platforms such as Facebook and Twitter should never be listed on resumes unless they are an example of an account you professionally operated. Facebook and Twitter profiles should be limited to personal acquaintances and family only – keep settings set to private or friends only. If utilized for professional purposes, Instagram is acceptable if showing photographic or design skills but should be limited to those uses only. Employers will view your social media presence, which might create a biased representation of who the applicant truly is and may mean the difference between employment or not.

Finally, do not include graphics within a resume. Some graphics will look basic or generic, drawing the attention away from content portrayed within your written narrative, or in general, just distracting. The practical mention of Human Resources hiring software or database noted above will also be greatly confused as the computer tries to process the information on the resume. [90]

Cenedella states toward the end of his writing that separate resumes should never be created when applying for a new position. He notes that this is a tedious task that requires great amounts of time – however, for the purposes of this writing, separate resumes, tailored to specific positions, should be created as it shows a willingness to put in the extra effort, the studious hard work that goes into researching a job posting is never a poor investment – remember, a big opportunity requires more than a small investment. [91]

As an example, I have included my resume for review. In 2019, AIA Kansas, or the American Institute of Architects Kansas Chapter, began their Young Architect of the Year Award, and I was the inaugural winner. You will see that my resume is drafted in a two-column layout

---

[90] Cenedella, 2019
[91] Cenedella, 2019

69

to show some artistic sensibilities while maintaining concise language and listing of education, employment, community involvement, and nonprofessional hobbies. This style deviates from some of the items noted above; however, the resume is strategically crafted to reflect my community involvement, professional contributions, and professional achievements, as the reviewing committee had stipulated. Always review any stipulations to postings or requests thoroughly before ever attempting to craft your resume or portfolio – their review committee will evaluate each component based on its relation to the guideline given, and sometimes any deviation may be grounds for dismissal of the candidate.

Creating a Portfolio

Young Me Moon's interesting take on consumers in her work, "*Different*," notes six different categories: category connoisseur, savvy opportunists, pragmatics, indifferent, reluctant, and brand loyalists.

1. Category Connoisseurs are experts in their field. They are highly selective, informed, and specific in their hiring practices[92] – inquire about the company's hiring practices, consult with past employees within your networks, discover if the business itself is self-aware and introspective – if so, they might fall under this category. (Art galleries or museums would possibly qualify under this category as they seek someone with a certain knowledge of the art industry).

2. Savvy Opportunists would be the type of hiring position where the managers or recruiters are less concerned about the person applying and more focused on the tasks and abilities of the

---

[92] Moon, 2011.

candidate.[93] With this, soft skills such as personability, punctuality, trustworthiness, and reliability are less a concern. Instead, the hiring manager focuses on the types of software a person can utilize, knowledge of equipment and ability to fix or repair the equipment, or other hard skills. (Professions such as this may include mechanics or IT professionals).

3. Pragmatics focus their energy on hiring someone without giving much consideration to the applicant but simply go through the interview process.[94] For instance, the company is more interested in a "warm body" to occupy a position such as a warehouse stocker or fast-food line preparation. (Businesses such as this may include Amazon's fulfillment centers).

4. Indifferent category types refer to a professional who hires someone simply to fill the position due to a lack of available labor within the market. Again, this category is much like the pragmatic in hiring a "warm body" to fill the position; a level of desperation might necessitate this category. (Following the pandemic, fast-food corporations such as McDonald's or Burger King have found themselves in the unfortunate position of not being able to hire employees that had made higher wages from unemployment benefits and are left with raising their wages significantly).

5. Reluctant employers might simply dread the interview process due to a former employee leaving abruptly or passing away.[95] In this scenario, it is doubtful that the new applicant will ever truly stand a chance of fulfilling their duties as well as the previous person. (This category arises at different times for nearly all industries that experience high turnover).

---

[93] Moon, 2011.

[94] Moon, 2011.

[95] Moon, 2011.

6. Brand Loyalists are those who truly are the company and who put forth every effort in finding the absolute best fit for their company and position.[96] (Business examples such as this include the hiring practices of Google or Alphabet).

Once you define these categories and investigate the hiring process, it's time to begin the planning stages. *"Different,"* notes where the connoisseur recognizes differences, the novice finds similarities, where the expert sees clear differences, the amateur cannot recognize the beginning, middle, or the end. Moon outlines ways of creating brands that can help you stand out for each of these categories: reverse brands, break away brands, hostile brands, confrontational and non-confrontational brands. [97]

The reverse brand will create a shift in perception for the consumer (in this case, your hiring manager).[98] In college, an individual, we will call him Brad, had access to a laser cutter and proceeded to laser cut a chess set – complete with box and playing instructions – and sent it to a prospective employer. Brad was applying for a position at a very hands-on design-build architecture firm, and he was able to completely standout from the other candidates by showing the firm how he could be creative, hands-on and design and build a three-dimensional chess set and playing instructions – that included his resume on the back of the playing instructions. Ultimately, he was able to reverse the typical concept of a resume and instead physically showed his capabilities – and then included the resume on the side. He got the job.

Breakaway brands create all new and alternative categories for the consumer.[99] My professional career has been somewhat of a breakaway brand. I worked on a design-build project during my fourth year at Kansas State University's College of Architecture, Planning, and

---

[96] Moon, 2011.
[97] Moon, 2011.
[98] Moon, 2011.
[99] Moon, 2011.

Design. The project was progressing slowly without much literal, concrete evidence. My professor introduced me to a local professional architect who brought me into work within his office. Instead of applying for a job to work on projects, I was able to bring the project to the employer and started work right away – I have now had the job for eight years.

Hostile brands simply state their case, good, bad, or indifferent, and don't care if the consumer likes it or not. These can be categorized further into confrontational or nonconfrontational brands.

When crafting a portfolio addressing the consumer category tailored toward your own personal brand, you may question the content to be included. Moon notes that brands often market *"product augmentation"* through means of increasing a set of benefits or skills of the person or product such as several years' experience working with a certain software[100] – versus *"augmentation by multiplication"* through increasing the quantity such as your own self-brand offering a skillset in three different computer programing platforms.[101] Here's an example, you can augment your product – you – by listing increased capacities within a company; then apply the principle of augmentation by multiplication by listing several tasks or duties fulfilled during that same time. For those with limited work experience, focus on a few skills and define them in more detail (product augmentation). For those with more experience, list concisely more skills or references (augmentation by multiplication). In any instance, only list items that can be expounded upon in an interview setting. Remember, don't disclose too much up front; a portfolio is best used as means of getting the interview, not in describing all the skills an applicant holds.

---

[100] Moon, 2011.
[101] Moon, 2011.

Sending a Resume and Portfolio

I was sitting at a folding table with a plastic top, metal fold-out legs, and an empty chair sitting directly across from me. A college-age woman in a mint-green sweater, hair neatly pulled back into a ponytail revealing gold and mint green earrings; she reached out her hand, perfectly polished mint green nail polish, and then proceeds to sit down, placing her portfolio and resume, stacked on the center of the table in front of us. To her right, she places a mint green sketchbook and a mint green pen on top. She gently rests her arms on the table, clasps her hands, and begins to tell me about herself. As she narrates her story, I look down and see that the resume was meticulously organized in a pleasing manner, with headings in mint green and latter paragraphs headlined in mint green as well. This impressed upon me the detailed character this candidate had. She had matched and strategized down to every minute detail, which had shown incredible attention to how serious the interview was and showed that she valued both our time.

Now that a resume and portfolio have been crafted, it is time to send your materials to prospective employers. First, save your files in the following format, as noted in *"Ladder's Resume Guide 2019"*:

Last Name. First Name. Resume/Portfolio. Year.pdf

It's worth noting that with more options available in the modern world, different word processing file types can be used. However, best practices would have the resume or portfolio saved as a .pdf, or Portable Document File. In saving and transmitting files in this format, the fonts, formatting, etc., all remain intact instead of having to be translated across foreign platforms. A .pdf file will be the best and most professional option. Once the file is saved, attach it to your professional email. In my own personal bias, if I receive a Word Document as an applicant's resume, I view it as a draft; a .pdf states that it is final, has been proofread, and is capable of presentation. In a subtle way, the applicant has shown that they have gone the extra mile to save it in the desired format and show their seriousness about becoming a professional within the business.

When applying for new jobs, applicants typically make one common major misstep: they fail to make contact prior to sending a resume and cover letter. Remember: always make contact prior to sending your materials. It can be in the form of a telephone call or an in-person meeting, which will put a voice or face to the applicant. Here, consider some of the themes written about in Adam Grant's best-selling book, "*Give and Take*," where he notes that weak ties, or people we are familiar with but do not know, introduce us to new leads. The initial phone call or face-to-face visit statistically offers a better chance of connecting you with your future employer. Grant details studies where he observed physicians who were provided with a photo of patients tended to have more accurate results in their diagnosis. The photograph helped create a personal connection and a visual of the impact of the physician's work. I'm not advocating including photographs within resumes or portfolios which may lead to unwanted or unintentional biases in the reviewer's deliberations; however, it is harder to say no to someone you have met versus a piece of paper on your desk.

Even if gainful employment is not achieved, it sets up an opportunity to create a dormant, or weak, tie; Grant notes these ties offer more novel information than current contacts. While a firm you interview at may not be hiring, they may refer you to another firm in town, that is. It is also worth noting that should an applicant ever find the need to reapply at that place of employment. Those dormant ties are easier to rekindle than starting anew each time. Take, for instance, Elizabeth Gilbert's short story: *Elk Talk*. Elizabeth became a household name with the meteoric rise of her novel "*Eat, Pray, Love*" and has experienced dormant ties and their benefits firsthand. In her book, "*Big Magic*," Gilbert tells the tale of a mischievous evening spent in Wyoming with a few drunk cowboys. As the night wore on, they began talking about elk mating calls – and it so happened that one of the cowboys had a tape recording of an expert elk caller. In an inebriated state of laughter, they wandered into the woods and began playing the elk call. A bull elk ran thundering in from nowhere and began stomping and pawing at the ground, trying to find the would-be competitor. Gilbert and the cowboy hid in the timber until the elk eventually left, and they wandered back to the ranch house with a newfound appreciation of nature. She goes on to explain that she wrote a short story titled "*Elk Talk*" and submitted it to a magazine company. The story ultimately was not published, and she received a courteous rejection letter in the mail. Following the success of her novel, "*Eat, Pray, Love,*" she resubmitted the short story ten years later to the same magazine. The editor remained in her role and contacted Gilbert immediately following the resubmission. The editor noted that she loved the story, and it reminded her of something; she just couldn't put her finger on it. Gilbert chuckles as she thinks to herself that the story reminds the editor of the story itself! This resubmission, ten years later, to "*Elk Talk*" being published for the world to read – never underestimate the power of dormant or weak ties and the impact they can have (try, try again).

Inevitably, applicants will find firms, corporations, or places of employment that simply are not hiring at the time of this initial contact. While discouraging, ask the company if they would be willing to sit down with you for a mock interview. While it takes time out of their schedule, it offers several benefits when the opportunity is taken. The applicant has the opportunity to sit through an interview, rehearse questions and practice responding while also allowing the interviewer the opportunity to practice asking questions, perfect their interview process – and create those weak ties, though they may become dormant, are useful, nonetheless. Grant's summary of advice-seeking in "*Give & Take*" could be applied here. He states that there are four benefits to a process like this one: learning, perspective-taking, commitment, and flattery.[102] Kansas State University's College of Architecture, Planning, and Design still offers this to their students and offers great opportunities to perfect skills and introduce professionals to potential candidates. Professionals can provide candid feedback in these settings because the outcome is not a hired position – but the distinct aspect of providing helpful feedback to the interviewer.

---

[102] Grant, 2014.

Section Summary

To build our career, resumes and portfolios are the initial steps in a lengthy process that leads to retirement. First, you must perform a self-inventory to define who you are, your personality, and how you work. In first understanding ourselves, we may begin to understand others – their personalities, how they work, and who they work best with. Your potential new employer will become the audience with which you will need to understand and find ways of communicating to connect your values with theirs.

Finding yourself and defining others will lead you on the path to defining your own journey and how you will reach this prospective audience. Outlining the steps needed and the people involved will allow you the opportunity to craft a resume and portfolio tailored specifically to everyone involved on a strategic course that aligns with the betterment of all parties involved. Script a narrative that vividly connects you with the employer, describes mutual goals, aspirations, and shared values that will make you stand out among the many, and lead the employer to choose you for the position. These narratives can be documented through resumes, portfolios, and interviews that increase awareness of your skills, personality, and work ethic.

Chapter 5: Networking 101

Things Always Come Full Circle

In our architecture firm, my business partner began working with a local church in 2002. As part of the project planning phases, he brought in a regional civil engineering firm as a consultant to design the landscaping, drainage plans, parking layouts, and other site amenities for the church project. Throughout the years, the project ebbed and flowed with interest, and twenty years later, the project is finally being constructed. During the two-decade time frame, the civil engineering firm needed to relocate their main offices due to a flooding incident that left their existing offices uninhabitable. The civil engineering firm asked our company to design their new offices due to the successful working relationship built while designing the church project. This relationship-building led to our firm being able to design a two million dollar building for the firm.

Circling back to the church project, one of the Arts & Architecture Committee board members referred our office to one of their close friends for a residential project. This referral brought us into the fold of designing a one-and-a-half-million-dollar residence for the close friend. My business partner also was invited to speak at a local sorority on campus – of which we had designed a two-million-dollar addition for the sorority corporation. During the speaking engagement, my business partner met a young lady that was a member of the sorority and the very same church we were designing. This young lady studied architecture and was seeking an internship, so we hired her. She also had a fiancé that was seeking employment, and she referred him to us, and we hired him too. From one single church project, the effects and networking relationships led to three-and-one-half-million dollars in construction projects and two new employees for us. Networking always comes full circle and can have benefits beyond our understanding.

Defining Networking

According to the U.S. Bureau of Labor Statistics, as quoted in James Citrin's *"The Career Playbook,"* 70% of all jobs were awarded to candidates through networking opportunities. His research surveyed young professionals specifically and found that 51% of individuals agreed with this statistic. Citrin's writings further define each category. He breaks it down through job fairs, references from hiring managers, meetings set up through peers and family members, and other means of networking. His findings reveal that 97% of young professionals surveyed – along with 100% of business professionals included in the study – noted that relationships in the business matter above all else. [103]

Before effectively networking, one must understand what exactly networking means. Marissa King's "*Social Chemistry*" notes that a networking connection begins as a *dyad* – meaning any two individuals who come together to bond within a one-on-one relationship. A dyad can consist of three types of networkers: expansionists, brokers, and conveners. Let's examine each type and consider which category you might fall into.[104]

Expansionists accumulate vast networks and are well known in several social circles. They have an innate ability to "work" a room – but on the other hand, they have trouble maintaining these networks due to the overall size and scope. With this trouble of regularly updating these networks, they have difficulty converting the relationships into benefits for themselves and others within their networks. Politicians often fall within this category as they embark on the campaign trail. They meet several people and occupy several networks and social circles but know little or nothing about those within the network.

Brokers have the ability to bring different groups together that typically occupy different realms or industries. With this ability, they can bring widely varied areas of knowledge and information and turn them into innovative benefits for themselves and their peers. One example of this is a "Referral Group." To illustrate how a referral group works, let us assume you need a new insurance agent to insure your car. You approach someone who belongs to a referral group, they introduce you to an

---

[103] Citrin, 2015.
[104] King, 2021.

insurance agent, and then you work with the agent to get your car insured. How this works is that the members of the referral group operate on an exclusive relationship – one insurance agent is present, one banker is present, one contractor is present, etc. – and any time someone needs one of these services, they have one person, and one person alone that they will refer you to.

Whereas expansionists prefer quantity, Conveners focus more on quality. By cohering to a quality network, conveners can build close-knit relationships that often include their friends and closest colleagues. Sometimes this dynamic may hamper the ability for differing views, but at the same time can develop highly understood sectors because of the specialized viewpoints. Local Chambers of Commerce would qualify for this category. The mission of many Chambers seeks to generate business attraction, retention, and growth and, therefore, will recommend quality businesses to one another for services or referrals. This builds a strong relationship between the Chamber and the businesses that comprise it. Chambers of Commerce also charge dues for membership leading to an atmosphere of businesses who can afford such a luxury. [105]

King describes that within these relationships, people have varying levels of social intelligence. Social intelligence revolves around two key factors, which include social awareness and social facility. Social awareness is our ability to see potential benefits in what we sense about others; the social facility is what we plan to do with this knowledge and how we begin to put these connections in motion. [106]

How then do we network and build these relationships? *"The Career Playbook"* outlines three simple steps for relationship building:

1. Reconnect with old friends and awaken dormant ties – this step is echoed in Adam Grant's *"Give & Take."*

---

[105] King, 2021.
[106] King, 2021.

2. Focus on your "Super Connectors."

3. Seek to help others.

Joining Young Professional or Emerging Professional organizations, industry associations, networking, or reference groups can allow you to "build your career when you're not building your career." [107] During these after-hours events, you can build quick acquaintances that at times fall dormant. Be sure to follow up with these dormant ties directly after meeting, or perhaps a week, month, or even a year after the meeting – this is how you can awaken dormant ties. If you question how these seemingly random conversations even begin, consider that in "*Social Chemistry*," King notes that each relationship begins as a dyad – two people interacting one-on-one. So, when attending an event, approach odd number groups to join or begin a conversation. Typically, two people will carry on a side conversation, and then the remaining person will turn to you to continue your own conversation – leading to a new connection! [108] (Since learning this technique, I have used it in social interactions and can attest, it's oddly satisfying and funny to watch).

The Law of a Few Sticky Connectors

Next, consider super connectors. In Malcolm Gladwell's "*The Tipping Point*," he notes the "Law of the Few" and the "Stickiness Factor." In the law of a few, we begin to understand that certain people play more of a role in a given process than others. Compound this law with the stickiness factor, and we can begin to see how networking or relationship building can quickly spread our reputation as well as provide references. To test the efficacy of the "Law of the Few," think back to when you

---

[107] Citrin, 2015.
[108] King, 2021.

were a child and played the game "telephone," where a group of people sits around a circle. One person starts the game by whispering a sentence or phrase into the ear of the person sitting next to them. This person, in turn, whispers this sentence to the person next to them; after a few people, the sentence begins to change meaning entirely. The initial sentence may have been that a pink elephant likes eating pineapple to a pink pineapple eating elephants. However, when a message contains a stickiness factor, those same few people begin to tell the same narrative, no matter how many participants there are. [109]

In the law of a few, look at who makes up the few: connectors, mavens, and salesman. Those who are connectors simply know a lot of people; their personalities allow them to interact with several different friends or acquaintance groups. Gladwell notes that most jobs come from these acquaintances because they simply occupy a different world than we do and have access to different information and connections. Mavens want to help and spread knowledge – applying this to when someone asks for a certain need fulfilled, i.e., a new receptionist, an attorney, or accountant. These mavens have accumulated knowledge of companies or position openings thanks in part to the connectors they interact with. Salesmen can pull others together with their ability to communicate. These types of employees work well when one needs to provide a reference or have a champion on your side – having someone sell your skillset versus advertising yourself speaks volumes. Gladwell notes that the more technology plays a role in the modern world, the more we will rely on primitive methods such as word of mouth. [110]

Why We Gather

After understanding the importance of networking, some of the key players, and how those within the network operate, we can look at effective means of building relationships and networking. For this topic,

---

[109] Gladwell, 2000.
[110] Gladwell, 2000.

we turn to *"The Art of Gathering: How We Meet and Why it Matters,"* by Priya Parker, which has been coined as a "Best Business Book" by several reputable publications.

Parker stresses that prior to any gathering or networking event, one must first decide why they are meeting. Are you networking or, more specifically, building trusting, quality relationships? Are you selling a product, or are you attempting to provide something that solves a problem for a potential audience? When we see gathering in this light, we understand that there is a difference between a category and purpose. Therefore, always seek out the purpose and remain steadfast to maintaining the objective or mission of the gathering. Once you know how important the purpose is, commit to the purpose. Parker provides the following tips for crafting a gathering's purpose: zoom out and look at the larger picture of why you are meeting; continually ask yourself why you are meeting; ask what the gathering can contribute to the greater good and work backward from this common goal to structure the gathering. [111]

Purpose also guides the conversation to align with the overall goal or mission of the meeting. Committing to one purpose and focusing on that singular purpose alone is paramount to creating clarity and achievement of the mission.

Fascinatingly, Parker emphasizes the importance of a purpose-driven list, meaning a list of those who need to be part of the gathering in terms of who to include and who to exclude. Only key individuals should be invited to drive the mission of the meeting; those who might complicate, or cause confusion should be excluded. The size of the gathering plays an important role in the efficacy of the congregating. Groups of less than eight individuals will limit diversity in ideas; however, a gathering that size creates an intimate, safe environment used to hone dedicated discussions. Gatherings of twelve to fifteen are focused enough to be facilitated by a single chair or leader but allow for more diverse ideas.

---

[111] Parker, 2020.

Groups of thirty begin to branch out and hold individual conversations and provide an energy of a party atmosphere. Groups of one hundred and fifty or smaller generate a "tribe" network, whereas anything larger becomes an audience or crowd. [112]

Is it important to determine who is there or who is not, but the choice of venue also carries an impact. Seek out a venue that signifies the framing of the gathering – formal, informal, energetic versus quiet, open, or intimate. The type of venue also contributes to the ability to create a defined perimeter to contain the meeting. Within the area or venue space, the density of people gathered forces the interactions in certain directions. However, an ad hoc gathering in an unpredictable location can have successful results as well. Parker also suggests that the success of a gathering or networking event begins the minute that attendees find out about the event. With that in mind, find ways of "priming" conversations or interactions well in advance of the meeting or gatherings so that relationships are set up before you attend, and then follow up shortly after the conclusion of the meeting to gauge its success. [113]

Section Summary

Through human evolution, social habits have formed and grown for the betterment of ourselves and others. Our networks keep us grounded, allow us to share ideas, and attain new avenues of thinking. Different types of people occupy these social circles, such as expansionists, brokers, conveners, connectors, mavens, and salesmen. They all play an integral role in the networks they help build and will benefit you if harnessed in meaningful ways. These meaningful ways can be guided through physical environments, those in attendance and a directed script to keep topics on task to pursue a purpose.

---

[112] Parker, 2020.
[113] Parker, 2020.

Chapter 6: Mastering the Interview

Selling Dirt to Cows

It was my second interview in two years. My FFA advisor had discussed the opportunity to interview for an Area I officer role in Savannah, Missouri. I took the chance and interviewed the first time, knowing full well I would not get a position due to my age. I was only a sophomore in high school, and officer positions were usually awarded to juniors who would serve during their senior year and prepare them for leadership roles in college. However, this was my second interview. I walked into the room with a navy-blue jacket and tie, and much to my surprise, the interviewers were the same as the previous year. As I stood there, hands clasped behind my back awaiting questions, I started to feel flushed but remembered the year before, and the thought of a second appearance calmed my nerves to an almost "what the hell, let's give this a try and see what happens," or in a more succinctly worded phrase, a cavalier mindset. The first portion of the interview is the same: "Tell us your name, a little about yourself, and your involvement in FFA."

"Good evening, everyone, my name is Garric Baker. I am a junior at Stanberry R-II, the son of a welder and a teacher, the youngest of two children. I have been involved with 4-H and FFA activities since I was eight years old and have come to learn the meaning behind dedication and hard work. Some of my FFA experiences have included competing locally and regionally in Soil Judging, Ag Sales, and Dairy Cattle Judging… so I guess you could say I can sell dirt to cows."

Immediately the entire panel cracked a grin or chuckled under their breath as they looked down at their papers and began making notes. My initial thought was, whoops, that last part wasn't prepared in advance, but then again, sometimes that's my authentic self of being a smart ass. After several rounds of interviews that evening, it finally came down to the announcement of the new slate of officers for the fall semester. They read the officer positions: historian, awarded to…, the sentinel, awarded to…, and the list went on. However, they started getting toward the top-tier positions, and they announced the two vice-presidential positions. My name was the only one that had not been called – and the dots immediately connected, "no way!" I thought to myself. "…and President of the Missouri Area I FFA Chapter for the 2007-2008 term: Garric Baker, Stanberry." How on earth did I pull that off? I was now slated to lead twenty-six FFA chapters in northwest Missouri.

This is one of my favorite stories to tell regarding interviews. I began authentically and honestly while remaining cognizant of the fact that I had returned a second time after knowing that my first attempt was a trial run for this moment. I was the only one to interview twice in two years. The preparation from the previous year showed my character and allowed me to connect and feel comfortable during the interview. Inevitably, everyone will endure interviews at some point in our lives, and preparation for these few moments is incredibly important.

Your Life Story

Following writing the resume, portfolio curation, and your eventual application submission, you will be called in for an interview. Look to Thea Kelley's "*Get That Job! The Quick & Complete Guide to a Winning Interview*," where she breaks down the interview process into simple categories to include noting what makes you stand out, harnessing the power of your stories, selling yourself, the power of practice, the importance of questions – asking and answering – nonverbal cues, and the follow up after the interview.

Kelley outlines the key pieces to the puzzle that is your life story. These pieces are your "R.E.V. Points" – Relevant, Exceptional, and Verifiable points that can assist you in educating your interviewer about who you are and why you are the best candidate for the job. Kelley notes that recent polls of business interviewers reveal that 50% of employers know within the first five minutes of the interview if you are a good fit for the company or not. With that being said, let's dive into the value of Kelley's R.E.V. Points and how you can develop them.[114]

Your R.E.V. Points are broken down into relevant, exceptional, and verifiable qualities. Your relevant qualities tend to be attributes that are in high demand by the employer; exceptional qualities help you to stand out from your peers and other candidates; finally, verifiable qualities are those that can be proven through credentials, evidence, records, or verification with past employers and references. [115]

Using these R.E.V. categories, you should develop a list of qualities. You can use these to build your resume but remember to develop these concepts further because the interviewer has already read it; now it is time to discuss who you truly are.

Kelley notes that a candidate will need a repertoire of approximately twenty to thirty stories to rely upon during interviews. Why? If appropriately short and concise, your personal stories allow interviewers opportunities to ask for additional details, which can lead to an authentic conversation. To construct your stories, use the SOAR method, meaning: Situation, Obstacle, Action, Result. The first principle of the SOAR method, situation, focuses on the who, what, where, and when of a given situation to provide context. This will allow your audience to paint a picture of the story and relate to obstacles you may or may not have overcome. Action points to your role in overcoming obstacles or reaching the desired destination. Without being too specific (unless asked), describe in just enough detail to show your competence level or your resolution. Finally, or to build up your story, place results at the beginning of your story. The results, numbers, quantities, and statistics provide credence to your story and capabilities. Kelley notes that this will give your story a "sound-bite."[116]

---

[114] Kelley, 2017.
[115] Kelley, 2017.
[116] Kelley, 2017.

Keep your stories under a minute or less. Practice if necessary. When you time yourself telling the story, avoid using a robotic tone; stick with a conversational tone. Doing so may help you realize how best to construct and deliver your narratives. If possible, ask the interviewer beforehand if there are any pre-planned questions, or review the most frequently asked questions, and if possible, find a way to connect your stories to these questions. If you have a predetermined list of questions or find typically asked questions online, these can act as valuable starting points in the development phase of crafting your stories.

Introductions

Now that your R.E.V. Points have been honed and your stories have been curated, it is time to consider how these are best implemented within the interview process. Here are the steps that Kelley recommends for a great R.E.V. introduction:

1. Get your answer off to a good start. Speak confidently as though you are conversing with a friend. Find a way to naturally weave your first R.E.V. Point into the introduction of the essential "Tell me about yourself" question. Again, remember that the interviewer will likely know if you will be a good fit within the first five minutes, so this part is critical.

2. Move on to your next R.E.V. Point building on the initial landing of your introduction.

3. Include examples for your points. This is where the verification part of R.E.V. can be further honed, hinting at your results, places to verify the claims, noting references, etc.

4. In this step, you will reveal even more about yourself, creatively interweaving your R.E.V. Points into your own character,

personality, and brief career summary, provided it is in a conversational tone and reveal a sense of humility in a brief amount of time.

5.   Remember to craft an ending to your introduction. The introduction will mean nothing unless a thorough, complete, and satisfying ending concludes the introduction.

The following steps are more preparatory for your delivery:

6.   Create an outline. A monotone delivery of a script sounds disingenuous, whereas talking points noted in an outline can help one deliver a conversational story.

7.   Practice your introduction and time yourself. This will allow you to "find your words" without stumbling through certain phrases, which can help keep your interviewer engaged by staying within a desirable time limit.

8.   Adjust your introduction as needed and as many times as necessary.

9.   Once you have practiced with your outline sufficiently, practice without it. This type of practice will help you deliver your introduction more naturally.

10. Finally, gain feedback from peers, mentors, friends, and family. Utilize this feedback and review your outlines once again to make any necessary changes. [117]

---

[117] Kelley, 2017.

Questions: Answering and Asking

With R.E.V. Points, stories, and introductions developed, candidates are recommended to work on the next phases of the interview, which Kelley identifies as: Questions, Answering and Asking. Not only are interviewers at this stage attempting to figure out if a candidate is a good fit for the company, but the candidate should also be interviewing the company to make sure that it is a good fit for themselves. This point is one of the most important steps in which many candidates often forget; all too often, we feel lucky and grateful for a job offer but putting this offer into perspective is crucial. Is the company a place where you would like to work for the next year? The next five years? Maybe ten?

Knowing that the candidate is just as important in the interviewing process as the interviewer, one can then begin to negotiate the aspects they consider important in their career trajectory. Kelley has the following recommendations to keep in mind to be authentic and strategic in your questions and answers. Provide real answers to questions that you find best suit the questions asked of you – but in turn, be strategic in asking questions of the company to find out the office culture, the priorities, and values of the business, etc.

Kelley identifies the "three C's" of interviewing: Competence, Compatibility, and Chemistry. Interviewers will want to figure out if you are competent for the position, compatible with the existing personalities within the office, and carrying the same values expressed as important to the business and chemistry between you and those around you. In turn, find out the competence level of your leaders – if you believe your manager to be competent, the more likely you will be to accept responsibilities and tasks in a civil manner; the compatibility – does their leadership styles and techniques align with your learning pattern? Finally, chemistry will allow you to determine if the place of business houses animosity or amiability. Many businesses today are struggling to hire individuals from the Millennial generation along with Gen-Xers and Gen-Z – and much of this is due to the reputations for poor workplace conditions. For instance, with the movement of work online, these latter generations have leverage over their place of work. The Boomer and Golden generations had to move to a location for a job – now, candidates can work remotely and remain in their place of choosing.[118]

Other recommendations include keeping your questions and answers clear, concise, and specific. You can then "listen between the lines," meaning to navigate your conversations – your interviewer will be doing the same – to determine if your answers are authentic and verifiable. Be sure to keep your answers and questions positive. If a company perceives that you hold negative emotions about your past employers, they may be hesitant to offer you a position with theirs. Finally, always remember that the interviewer wants you to succeed – after all, if you succeed, you get the job, they get a great employee, the business benefits, customers receive improved products or services, and effective interview has led to a great working relationship for all. Suppose you don't succeed at the interview. In that case, the interviewer must readvertise the position, interview another pool of candidates, lose valuable time that could be spent working on other responsibilities – so it is in their best interest for you to succeed.

Rounding out Kelley's recommendations "nailing the nonverbals." Put simply, eye contact should be kept to approximately 30-60% of the time during the interview. Any less seems disingenuous, and more seems off-putting. Smiling during the interview should be kept to times when it feels natural; however, do not smile when you feel nervous or awkward because you can smile too much during an interview. When shaking hands – be respectful of the recipient; be firm without being too powerful as some have less tolerance to overly aggressive handshakes. Limit gestures, speak in a moderate tone that uses variation that matches your narratives without going to extremes, mirror the body language of your interviewer, listen, and take notes if allowed within the meeting are all additional tips to help win over the interviewer. Be sure to check your appearance prior to exiting your home for the interview. Your clothing

---

[118] Kelley, 2017.

will speak for you when entering a parking lot, building, lobby, office space, or wherever and provides that crucial first impression.[119]

Closing the Interview

Once you have succeeded at landing and performing your interview, close by showing appreciation for the opportunity to interview, summarize your R.E.V. Points, express your interest in obtaining the position, and keep closing thoughts to a minute or less. Finally, make notes in your car or commute following the interview. These notes will help you remember areas you excelled at, areas to improve upon, as well as additional follow-up questions you may have. Follow up with an email thanking the company for the opportunity, which will show your continued interest in the job opportunity and hopefully keep your name at the front of the candidate pool.

Section Summary

Compelling life stories make for wonderful introductions when interviewing. However, asking and answering questions will reveal a multitude of information about a prospective employer. The candidate being interviewed is just as important as the company performing the interviews. Successful working relationships are started through effective interviews – and that we must remember, there are no bad employees, just misguided interviews. If a person is hired and the working relationship turns less than productive, neither party is at fault, but the process of the initial interview failed to reveal valuable information for the parties involved. Had better questions and answers been asked and given, the two may have amicably decided to part ways earlier in the process and allowed a better match to take place and create outstanding results.

---

[119] Kelley, 2017.

Chapter 7: Employee Development

Why Employee Development

Employee development is crucial in building a career as well as enhancing productivity and results within a company. In their work, *"Built to Last: Successful Habits of Visionary Companies,"* Jim Collins and Jerry Porras evaluated eighteen case studies of visionary companies – sixteen of which had a driven focus on employee development that far exceeded their counterparts. One way to measure the success of a company or firm's employee development, *"It's The Manager"* authors Jim Clifton and Jim Harter, note when an organization is polled and more than 60% of their employees can agree with the following statement, the company is one of high development: "There is someone at work who encourages my development." [120]

What then is employee development? To many, it will have a different definition. In *"Watch Them Grow or Watch Them Go,"* Beverly Kay and Julie Winkle-Guilioni define it as, "development is nothing more than helping others grow and nothing less." It all boils down to quality conversations.[121] These conversations can take place with yourself, trusted friends, colleagues, and eventually your employer. *"It's The Manager"* indicates that career or employee growth and opportunities are the number one reason people change jobs.[122] How then can we describe in more specific terms what these growth opportunities look like? Gallup's findings state that the following three factors contribute to an employee's definition of growth opportunities: fit with career aspirations, opportunity to make a difference, and success.[123]

"It's The Manager" authors note that the first step in developing employees, managers, and leadership teams is to run an audit on all learning opportunities and evaluate these opportunities to ensure they are building a strengths-based culture. To begin an evaluation of your current development, an employee's current development, or even a

---

[120] Clifton & Harter, 2019.
[121] Kaye & Giulioni, 2019.
[122] Clifton & Harter, 2019.
[123] Clifton & Harter, 2019.

team's current development, *"It's The Manager"* recommends asking these eight questions:

1. What are your recent successes?

2. What are you most proud of?

3. What rewards and recognition matter most to you?

4. How does your role make a difference?

5. How would you like to make a bigger difference?

6. How are you using your strengths?

7. How would you like to use your strengths moving forward?

8. What knowledge would you like to gain? [124]

Question one, what are your recent successes, can be approached from many perspectives. As an emerging professional, what have been your recent successes or accomplishments both professionally and personally? From a manager's perspective, list the accomplishments of your employees, your managers, and then lastly yourself. Grant's *"Give & Take"* states that individuals are more likely to recognize the contributions of others when taking stock of their contributions before listing their own, which may generate an unwanted bias and inflate our own contributions. [125]

The second question, as a young professional, what are you most proud of, consider the role of the manager and what are your employees most proud of, and what are you most proud of regarding your team, even your own career? The third question requires a deeper introspective look at

---

[124] Clifton & Harter, 2019.
[125] Grant, 2014.

what motivates an individual, what types of recognition and rewards matter most, and which provide a greater sense of accomplishment. Do you find some as hollow acknowledgments or genuine praise?

When it comes to praise, there are many aspects that everyone should consider. Gary Chapman states that there are several languages of appreciation – especially in the workplace. "*The 5 Languages of Appreciation in the Workplace*" breaks the concept down into two categories: primary and secondary forms of appreciation – everyone has their own primary form of acceptance and appreciation. The different subcategories of appreciation include quality time, words of affirmation, acts of service, tangible rewards, and physical touch. Each employee will have a primary form of appreciation, followed by a secondary form of appreciation, both of the five subcategories.[126]

Before defining each subcategory, let us examine why appreciation is a good investment. In Chapman's studies, 81% of respondents noted that they were more likely to try harder when their immediate managers showed some form of appreciation. When employees try harder, they become more engaged, and as a result, these employees are 27% less likely to miss days for illness, have 27% higher customer service ratings, they are 18% more productive, and even 22% more profitable. On the other hand, disengaged employees are 51% more likely to experience turnover, 62% more likely to have an accident on the job, and companies even lose 51% more of their inventory due to employee theft.[127]

According to Chapman's studies, employee turnover is estimated to cost American businesses nearly $5 trillion annually – and 66% of employees said they would quit if they did not feel appreciated in the workplace. Financial incentives,

---

[126] Chapman, 2007.
[127] Chapman, 2007.

or what Chapman calls extrinsic rewards, only accounted for 2% of the motivation to work. Intrinsic rewards, such as one of the five languages of appreciation, accounted for far more in retaining employees. Here are the five appreciation languages:[128]

1. Words of Affirmation. This type of appreciation occurs when managers verbally praise their direct reports, and this praise must be specific and individualized to each employee based on their character traits and accomplishments. These words can also be spoken privately or publicly, depending on the employee's preference.

2. Quality Time. Undivided time between the direct report and a manager allows both parties to have shared experiences and gives the employee the feeling or sense of simply being included as part of the team.

3. Acts of Service. An act of service for the employee consists of doing something kind or thoughtful that benefits the recipient.

4. Tangible Rewards. Gifts such as food, gift cards, certificates, and other tangible items are typically the least useful types of appreciation. However, experiences such as movie tickets or tickets to a sporting event, or time off can be more effective than tangible rewards.

5. Physical touch, as Chapman notes it, can be controversial. However, there are noncontroversial forms of touching that can be used that include fist bumps, handshakes, or high-fives.

---

[128] Chapman, 2007.

Discover your own primary and secondary forms of appreciation – and if you are a manager, determine the types of appreciation your employees respond best to – and this will increase your engagement within the workplace. It's also important to note the difference between appreciation and recognition. Chapman states that recognition looks at the employee's performance, whereas appreciation looks at the value of the individual. Recognition looks at what someone does, while appreciation looks at who the person is. [129]

The fourth and fifth questions determine areas you feel employees and teammates may feel that they are contributing or leaving a lasting impact. The final three questions take into account the person's strengths, where they are effectively and efficiently utilized, areas for those skills to excel, and areas where these strengths can be nurtured.

Gallup's research found that only one in three employees or managers have been offered a growth opportunity within the last year. In "*Help Them Grow or Watch Them Go*," Kaye and Winkle-Giulioni highlight three key conversations that need to occur to start, or to refresh, one's career and employee development: hindsight conversations, foresight conversations, and the culmination of the two for an insightful conversation. The hindsight conversations reflect on their past accomplishments, positions, strengths, and weaknesses. Once someone has established a hindsight conversation, the discussion can morph into a foresight conversation. Within a foresight conversation, one must look forward to what can be new opportunities, areas to grow strengths, and reduce weaknesses. Combine the two for an insightful conversation to formulate a plan of action, taking past accomplishments and

---

[129] Chapman, 2007.

achievements and weighing them against new opportunities and positions.[130]

How, then, does one go about laying out these conversations? Kaye and Winkle-Giulioni recommend the following approach for establishing a hindsight conversation:

1. The initial discussion should revolve around listing past accomplishments, achievements, experiences, job positions, organizational involvement, etc., to discover any common themes and trends.

2. Next, ask yourself, or your employee, or employer, where you were happiest, excelled the most, struggled the most, or simply lost interest.

3. Throughout the process note and evaluate themes and trends that emerge. [131]

This initial conversation should be had regularly, possibly as part of an employee review, but try not to confuse performance with the overall discussion. Additional benefits may be found when having a conversation with coworkers, friends, or trusted advisors prior to having this discussion with your employer. Ideas or the discovered themes may be solidified when viewed from several perspectives – including your own. [132]

Another theory that reinforces the importance of the conversation shown above is referenced in *"It's The Manager."* These conversations should be less of an employee review and considered more as a form of coaching. Gallup notes five types of coaching conversations: 1. role and

---

[130] Kaye & Giulioni, 2019.
[131] Kaye & Giulioni, 2019.
[132] Kaye & Giulioni, 2019.

relationship orientation, 2. the quick connect, 3. the check-in, 4. developmental coaching (which would be where the hindsight, foresight, and combination conversations noted above would be categorized), and 5. progress reviews. [133]

Kaye and Winkle-Giulioni propose that career development is, in essence, a deal made between an employer and employee in their phrasing of "let's make a DEAL." It's a clever acronym outlining that the career development plan must be Documented, Employee-owned, Aligned with employee goals, and Linked to the organization's needs. In the documentation, write down the career development plan to solidify and make official the intent of the processes and outcomes of the development as well as a means of measuring success in the development. This plan must also be employee-owned so that the employee, or in this case, our reader, can take pride and ownership of the process. Alignment with personal and professional goals must also be integral to the plan. The final letter of the acronym links the plan to the needs of the organization or company because resources in business are often limited and must be spent wisely. [134]

Kaye and Winkle-Giulioni also identify another clever acronym: ESP – Ever-Scanning and Pondering. This thought process will enable the reader to generate a forward-thinking perspective. Their steps for starting an ESP mindset go something like this: interview key individuals, engage in focused customer contact, research important issues or trends, read trade publications, participate in industry conferences, and attend management or other cross-discipline meetings. [135]

Another key concept that the authors present is the professional ladder doesn't always lead up: instead of a ladder, think of corporate hierarchy as a rock wall. Professionals may not always seek to move upward within a company; some may wish to move laterally, thereby learning several aspects of the business or company and further cementing their place in

---

[133] Kaye & Giulioni, 2019.
[134] Kaye & Giulioni, 2019.
[135] Kaye & Giulioni, 2019.

it. A novel idea for firms would see the extinction of job titles. A person's title within a company limits their abilities to a predefined position whereas a person without a title can grow their abilities and the position they hold. [136]

Another form of employee or career development, the authors note, comes from the Cisco Connected Learning Experience. Cisco's methodology presents three E's: Education, Exposure, and Experience. They describe that education should be multi-modal and open to different and new opportunities. Their guidance notes that expectations should be set in advance of educational opportunities to foster intentional learning. Once time has been set aside for the reader to learn, preserve that time for learning. Following the education portion, put it to use and debrief following the real-world application of lessons. The second E, exposure, allows employees, or yourself, the opportunity to learn from a new mentor by being exposed to different ways of thinking and applications. The final E, experience, mixes intention and attention. Subjects should find intentional and sometimes nonintentional experiences, all the while paying close attention to learning opportunities. [137]

Building on the idea of employee development, turn to growing talent. Daniel Coyle, author of *"The Little Book of Talent: 52 Tips for Improving Your Skill,"* and *"The Talent Code: Talent Isn't Born, It's Grown,"* has taken an incredibly detailed look at how to harness the power of growing our own talents. His books outline the following tips for improving your skillset (read *"The Little Book of Talent"* for a complete, descriptive listing):

1. Stare at Who You Want to Become: A simple connection with a role model can increase your unconscious motivation. Studies found that individuals who were told they share a birthday with

---

[136] Kaye & Giulioni, 2019.
[137] Kaye & Giulioni, 2019.

a famous mathematician improved their willingness to put forth effort into a difficult math problem by an astounding 62%.[138]

2. Engrave the Skill You Want to Develop: Spend at least fifteen minutes daily attempting to engrave the skill in your mind. [139]

3. Steal without Apology: For this one technique, I will reference a term I learned while volunteering on an economic committee – R&D. Often, we think of R&D as Research and Development, but for Coyle's technique, it could also represent Rip-off and Duplicate. Find what is working well for others and duplicate it yourself. Taking that same term further, consider it as Refine and Develop. Take these skills and continually fine-tune each one to fit your objective. [140]

4. Buy a Notebook: Keep a journal of your experiences and moments of growth. We are visual animals; simply seeing your progress or word and sketches committed to paper will give you a sense of accomplishment. By viewing your markings on a page and slowly accumulating more, you will become biased that you are growing, and this perceived growth compounds to continued growth both real and perceived. [141]

5. Be Willing to Be Stupid: This is one of my favorite techniques and provided one of my own breakthroughs within my career. We all know something that someone else doesn't. We cannot be afraid of looking stupid or uninformed, but you can ask questions or attempt something new and seek feedback. We are all learning. [142]

---

[138] Coyle, 2012.
[139] Coyle, 2012.
[140] Coyle, 2012.
[141] Coyle, 2012.
[142] Coyle, 2012.

6. Choose Spartan Over Luxurious: Whenever possible, choose the simple, basic path. When we lavish ourselves with materialistic things, we often confuse ourselves by thinking we have "made it." Continually stay within your growth mindset.[143]

7. Before You Start, Figure Out What Type of Skill It Is: Hard skills and soft skills require different types of implementations. Coyle notes that hard skills require the ABC Method – Always Be Consistent. These skills require repetition and accuracy, whereas soft skills require flexibility and the three R's – reading, recognizing, and reacting. Most skills combine the two and require different learning methods but still carry weight in your personal growth. [144]

8. Five Ways to Pick a High-Quality Teacher or Coach: avoid someone who accommodates your every need, seek someone who may even scare or intimidate you to some extent, seek an individual who provides short, clear directions, find a mentor who loves teaching fundamental ideas, and when in doubt, work with someone older – they have experience and knowledge gained simply by being in the industry longer. [145]

9. Take Off Your Watch: Try not to focus on the time a task or skill takes to acquire. Instead, focus on successful attempts so that you unconsciously train yourself to notice the correct ways of accomplishing something and implementing it earlier in the process, allowing those successful attempts with more frequency.

10. Break Every Move Down into Chunks: Much like the Lao Tzu quote, "A journey of a thousand miles begins with one step," you should break down each task into a manageable,

---

[143] Coyle, 2012.
[144] Coyle, 2012.
[145] Coyle, 2012.

measurable piece and work on perfecting the skill. From there, move on to the next individual piece, and before too long, several perfect pieces have a well-rounded outcome seamlessly fitting together. Each day, focus on building a perfect piece of your new skill as a starting point. [146]

11. Embrace Struggle: No one ever grew in their comfort zone. Seek out the struggle it takes to harness a new skill and embrace it. Within the struggle, focus on five minutes of deep practice without interruption. By focusing on this short burst of perfection, we tune our mindset to focusing on the correct methods instead of spending countless hours of indirect practice. [147]

12. Practice Alone: Deep practice works best in smaller, confined spaces where the individual is alone and progressing at their own pace. [148]

13. Stop Before You are Exhausted: A tired individual learns at a significantly slower pace than one who is well-rested and energized to learn. [149]

14. End on a Positive Note: Finally, Coyle recommends ending on a positive note. Reward yourself, compliment yourself; however, you choose to end on a positive note, this practice will help grow your motivation and increase your overall drive to accomplish the skill. [150]

---

[146] Coyle, 2012.
[147] Coyle, 2012.
[148] Coyle, 2012.
[149] Coyle, 2012.
[150] Coyle, 2012.

Section Summary

Once a career has been found, employees and managers should continue to grow their own skillsets and understanding of those around them through employee development. Careers may turn stagnant over time and lead to disengaged employees – or worse, employees actively detracting from the business. However, in understanding several contributing factors that include our own successes, achievements, languages of appreciation, and how employees can make meaningful strides in our professions, a Young Professional can begin their career and grow it to a prosperous and satisfying endeavor. Included at the end of this section is a sample Young Professional's Checklist for a documented, employee-owned plan that can be aligned to your own goals and linked to the goals of the organization in which you work.

Conversations between employee and manager can lead to breakthrough ideas, autonomy, ownership within a career, and learning opportunities. These conversations will reveal past accomplishments and strengths, and these areas of excellence may not always lead up the corporate ladder but hopscotch to better align with the employees' own personal goals for the betterment of the company. In these conversations, figure out who you want to become, how to get there, what skills will be needed, and find mentors and teachers along the way. Harness different strategies to hone new skills and foster a growth mindset to find more fulfillment within your own employee development journey.

YOUNG PROFESSIONALS
HANDBOOK CHECKLIST

YOUNG PROFESSIONAL CHECKLIST

Name: _____

Address: _____ State:_____ Zip: _____

Phone Number: (___) ____ - _____

Email Address: _____

Education & Credentials:

Institution: _____

Degree:
- O H.S. Diploma/GED   O Some College
- O Associates   O Bachelors
- O Masters   O Doctorate

Year Obtained: _____

Career Phase:
- O Aspiration Phase   O Promise Phase
- O Experience Phase   O Harvest Phase
- O Encore Phase   O Legacy Phase

Aspiration Phase:

The mission of my aspiration phase is to prepare my selfbranded material in hopes of obtaining an interview following graduation or credentialling.

First Point of Contact
- O Screener   O Recruiter
- O Hiring Manager   O Human Resources

Creating a Resume
- O Start w/ blank doc O Contact Info
- O Prof. Summary   O Experience
- O Education   O Clear format
- O Proofread   O Saved as .pdf

I will be submitting my resume to:

Name: _____

Job Title:_____

Phone Number: (___) ____ - _____

Email Address: _____

- O *I have made contact prior to sending materials.*
- O *I have included a cover letter.*

Promise Phase:

The mission of my promise phase is to network more, engage in a successful interview, and obtain gainful employment at a position I can grow professionally.

Organizations I am involved in and can network in include:

1) _____

2) _____

3) _____

4) _____

5) _____

I will be interviewing with:

Name: _____

Job Title:_____

Phone Number: (_____) _____ - _____

Email Address: _____

○ *I have confirmed the date of the interview.*
○ *I have sent a thank you or follow up correspondence following the interview.*

Interview   ○ Casual   ○ Business Casual
  Attire   ○ Professional

Interview Date: _____   Interview Time: _____

I have been made an offer of employment:
○ *I have acknowledged the offer.*
○ *I have negotiated the offer.*
○ *I have accepted the offer.*
○ *I have confirmed start dates, attire*
   expectations, other negotiated items.

Experience Phase:

The mission of my experience phase is to utilize my credentials earned in the aspirational phase, embrace the promise granted to me, and grow my experience.

My recent accomplishments include:

1) _____
2) _____
3) _____

I am most proud of:

1) _____
2) _____
3) _____

My rewards and recognitions include:

1) _____
2) _____
3) _____

My role makes a difference by:

1) _____
2) _____
3) _____

I would like to make a bigger difference by:

1) _____
2) _____
3) _____

I am using my strengths by:

1) _____
2) _____
3) _____

I would like to use my strengths moving forward by:

1) _____

2) _____

3) _____

Knowledge I would like to gain includes:

1) _____

2) _____

3) _____

Someone within my career cares about my future; this person is:

Name: _____

Job Title: _____

Someone I consider a mentor is:

Name: _____

Job Title: _____

I have had the following conversations this year on a regular basis:

Needed Conversations	O Hindsight	O Insight
	O Foresight	O Human Resources

Coaching Conversations	O Role & Relationships
	O Quick Connect
	O Check-In
	O Developmental
	O Progress Reviews

I have contributed to the following retirement plan

O 401k   O Simple IRA

O Money Market   O ROTH IRA

Harvest Phase:

The mission of my harvest phase is to foster effective communication, grow my teams, and continue my learning trajectory.

The following team members are Thinkers:

1) _____

2) _____

3) _____

The following team members are Imaginers:

1) _____

2) _____

3) _____

The following team members are Persisters:

1) _____

2) _____

3) _____

The following team members are Rebels:

1) _____

2) _____

3) _____

The following team members are Harmonizers:

1) _____

2) _____

3) _____

The following team members are Promoters:

1) _____

2) _____

3) _____

The following team members are Innovators:

1) _____

2) _____

3) _____

The following team members are Late Adopters:

1) _____

2) _____

3) _____

The following team members are Early Adopters:

1) _____

2) _____

3) _____

The following team members are Laggards:

1) _____

2) _____

3) _____

I have had the following conversations this year on a regular basis with my teammates:

Needed
Conversations

○ Hindsight
○ Foresight

○ Insight
○ Human Resources

Coaching
Conversations

○ Role & Relationships
○ Quick Connect
○ Check-In
○ Developmental
○ Progress Reviews

My diverse team includes the following:

○ Women
○ Different Races

○ LGBTQ+ Community
○ Generational Diversity

Encore Phase:

The mission of my encore phase is to train my replacement, establish a transition plan, evaluate my finances, and train my successors for a successful retirement.

In planning for my retirement I have done the following:

○ Business Plan
○ Succession Plan

○ Trained my Successor(s)
○ Evaluated Finances

I mentor the following people:

Name: _____

Job Title: _____

Name: _____

Job Title: _____

Name: _____

Job Title: _____

Name: _____

Job Title: _____

Legacy Phase:

The mission of my legacy phase is to help train future generations, give back to my community, and contribute to philantrhopic ventures.

I volunteer at the following organizations:

1) _____

2) _____

3) _____

I donate to the following organizations:

1) _____

2) _____

3) _____

I provide mentorship to the following people:

1) _____

2) _____

3) _____

I reside on the following committees/boards:

1) _____

2) _____

3) _____

Chapter 8: Difficult Conversations

Sometimes You Have to Shake a Few Trees

In the mid-1800s, the Guenther family traveled across the Atlantic in hopes of finding a better life in America. They first settled in Wisconsin, then later traveled to a rural area of northwest Missouri, which they came to call home. They built a rough-looking wood shack as a house. Around the late 1800s, the Red Delicious Apple was making waves through the agriculture industry as the best new produce tree to plant. The Guenther's set out and planted incredible orchards of various apple trees, walnut trees, peach and pear trees, gooseberry bushes, cherry trees, grape vines – they had a wide variety to tend to. Fast forward roughly 100 years, and my grandfather – standing at 6' tall with his stark white hair, bifocals, and an ornery grin that revealed itself every now and again – had his own small orchard. He mainly grew walnut trees and sold the walnuts by the truck load. One afternoon, my mother and I, this was when I was about eight years old, headed to my grandparent's house to help my grandfather pick up walnuts.

When we arrived, Grandma proceeded to tell us that the walnuts had not fallen yet, "and I don't know where Bob went..." (she never called him "Grandpa" or "Granddad," just Bob... unless she was upset with him, then it was "Robert!"), but that "he was out there puttering around on his tractor." My mother and I went outside to see my grandfather, bouncing in the old flat metal seat as the tractor popped and smoked its way over to one of the largest walnut trees, which happened to be nearest the house. He backed the tractor under the tree, climbed down, and adjusted a 6' snow pushing blade that was attached to the tractor, climbed back on the tractor, and looked over at my mother and me. One thing to know about Grandpa is that he had a silver crown put on one of his back teeth at some point in his life, and if he smiled just enough, his smile literally shimmered a little.

As he sat atop the tractor, he looked at my mother and me... and he smiled his ornery, shimmering grin as he slid his foot from the brake and the clutch simultaneously. The tractor popped and jolted back and rammed the tree. The leaves at the top shook and vibrated as the walnuts fell all around my smiling Grandpa. To conclude the story, we picked up a full truck load of walnuts and took them to market. As an eight-year-old boy, I got a $57 check, a smile on my face, an afternoon with my family, and a lifelong lesson: sometimes, to get what you want – you have to shake a few trees.

When asking for a raise or an advance on your pay, several factors need to be considered. First, let us begin with understanding the division of labor as described prior to Durkheim's definition and the advent of money following a trading and bartering society that built wealth among nations and their inhabitants.

The Wealth of Nations, Built by the Hands of Others

Adam Smith authored "*The Wealth of Nations*" over a span of ten years in the late 1700s. In the first book, Smith examines the division of labor and the origins of the use of money. Smith's definition of the division of labor, preceding Durkheim's, states that distinct hands perform distinct divisions of labor – sometimes, the hands of many create more than the hands of a few. This separation of labor, or what became known as trades, creates more output. He notes that there are three aspects of the division of labor: improved dexterity of every particular worker, the saving of time usually lost when transferring from one type of work to another, and the invention of machines facilitate and abridge labor to allow the work of one man to be greater than many. Smith posits that this division of labor is a gradual consequence of human nature in that self-interest drives humans to trade or barter one thing for another. This is dictated by the market: when the market is small, no single person should be given reign over the ownership of all trades because it creates a monopoly; in contrast, when the market is large, the division of labor then balances itself with the high number of tradesmen. [151]

---

[151] Smith, 2011.

All this trading and bartering by several individuals gave way to a need to measure such transactions. Smith provides an example where the butcher does not take his meat to the baker to exchange for bread; instead, he takes his meat to the marketplace, trades this for some form of compensation – the advent of money allowed for tradesmen's wares to be easily carried in forms of silver, gold, and copper. These pieces of metal could then be taken to the baker and traded for bread. A surplus in these wares or produce allowed the individual to become a merchant himself, whereas those who had no produce or goods to trade, or barter could then offer themselves through labor to help the merchant create more produce. The merchant can then trade pieces of silver and gold for the labor of others and gives those with nothing something to trade for goods. This led to the universal use of some type of monetary trade. [152]

The divisions of labor created divisions in labor classes. Those with the ability to become merchants or of higher status set themselves apart from those who lacked the ability to grow their own skillsets. Smith notes that the lower class becomes increasingly larger as this unqualified workforce continues to grow. Smith also presents five factors that impact labor and the divisions of labor. The first consists of the agreeableness and disagreeableness of the employees – how likely are the laborers to give themselves up to do the work. The second factor is the ease and cheapness, or the difficulty and expense of learning – laborers may be trained in a day, whereas those requiring higher degrees or competencies in a field must undertake the expenses to learn these skills. The third component is the consistency and inconsistency of employment in them – seasonal labor forces or other factors that drive the continuity of work impacts the division in some labor sectors. Fourth, the level of trust that must be imposed on those that exercise them, and fifth, the probability or improbability of success in them. These last two factors indicate whether the workforce can succeed and find stability within the division of labor they are employed. [153]

---

[152] Smith, 2011.
[153] Smith, 2011.

Wages, A Simple Understanding

Stephen J. Dubner and Steven D. Levitt give us a much simpler view of how wages are determined for a given profession in their book, "*Freakonomics.*" The first rule, understandably, states that the specialized requirements and skill sets will greatly impact the qualifications, whether secondary education or technical skills and therefore be reflected in the wages paid (This applies to Smith's "ease or cheapness, difficulty and expense of learning"). The second factor can be summed up with the basic knowledge of supply and demand – how many job applicants are available and willing to fill the positions (Smith's Consistency and inconsistency of employment in them"). The third factor is the unpleasantness of the job or duties fulfilled from the position (Smith's "Agreeableness and disagreeableness"). Finally, the fourth factor, demand for services needing to be provided, round out the typical contributors to the determination of a wage[154] (Smith's "Level of trust," and "the probability or improbability of success in them").

Gender and Inequality

The modern era recognizes that gender and pay inequality exists – yet few understand the depths of the inequality and the overarching impact that the pay gap has on society. Craig Wright, Ph.D., in his book, "*The Hidden Habit of Genius,*" recites statistics given in a 2019 study, "*Prejudice Against Women Leaders,*" in which 1,529 respondents, men, and women, held biases against women leaders. Of the male respondents, 36% held prejudiced views of women leaders – but more surprisingly, 10% of women also held these same views. Another statistic Dr. Craig provides comes from "*Sex and Gender in the 2016 Presidential Election,*" which revealed that a majority of men looked unfavorably on power-seeking women, whereas 30% of women also looked unfavorably on women leaders.[155] Yale psychologists administered an experiment in

---

[154] Levitt & Dubner, 2014.
[155] Wright, 2020.

2012 where a fictitious CV (curriculum vitae) was distributed for a managerial position in a science lab. The CV was distributed to part of the reviewing participants with a male name, and the remaining respondents received a CV with a female name. Unfortunately, the experiment showed that the reviewing participants favored the male candidate more than the female, was deemed more suited for the position, and worthy of a higher salary with mentoring options. Even more disappointingly, the reviewers were both men and women and shared equally unfavorable views of the female candidate.[156] Professor Dean Keith Simonton and his book *"Greatness: Who Makes History and Why"* posits that for one identifiable female genius, it is possible to name ten male geniuses. Women have often been overlooked for their contributions throughout history and have been compensated even less than their male counterparts.[157]

In Kathy Caprino's *"The Most Powerful You: 7 Bravery-Boosting Paths to Career Bliss,"* she notes that 57% of employees have never negotiated their salary. [158] Adam Grant's *"Give & Take"* suggests that one of the main reasons for gender pay inequality is that men are eight times more likely to negotiate their wages. Conversely, Caprino notes that gender bias is real and has more of an impact on women. She notes that women who ask for what they want or attempt to negotiate for a higher salary are perceived as being "assertive and forceful," thereby causing a perceived drop in competency by 35% at the cost of a lost $15,000 – in contrast to men's competency only dropping 22% and limited to a financial loss of $7,000 when they are viewed in the same manner. [159]

Young Professionals in the future will also be the most diverse they have ever been – Dr. Stefanie K. Johnson, Ph.D., and writer of *"Inclusify: The Power of Uniqueness and Belonging to Build Innovative Teams,"* notes that 51% of the population in the United States (at the time of her writing in 2019) are women and 39% minorities. Dr. Johnson describes the

---

[156] Wright, 2020.
[157] Wright, 2020.
[158] Caprino, 2020.
[159] Caprino, 2020.

concept of Inclusify as the action of embracing different backgrounds to piece teams together around a common purpose. Her clever equation is noted as follows: uniqueness + belonging = inclusion.[160]

Dr. Johnson notes that one of the barriers dissuading real inclusion is caused by unconscious bias. She cites a study of 1,918 people, in which the participants who felt perceived bias against them were three times as likely to be disengaged at work, twice as likely to feel angry or upset in the workplace, and only half as likely to feel pride in their organization. To punctuate and emphasize the importance of the study, it revealed that the same participants were three times as likely to quit their job. Ways of combating unconscious bias are through practicing Dr. Johnson's "ABC's of Breaking Bias:

> **A** - Acknowledge that everyone has unconscious bias. If you read this and thought that you were not biased, guess again – it is unconscious, so of course, you do not think you are biased.

> **B** – Block any opportunities for bias. Whenever selecting applicants, people for your teams; block names to decrease and remove bias completely from the model.

> **C** – Count it. Find a way of setting milestones within your teams, companies, or organizations to increase diversity and create opportunities for inclusion. [161]

---

[160] Johnson, 2020.
[161] Johnson, 2020.

As professions become more diverse, companies and organizations can work to embrace inclusion. In *"Inclusify,"* Dr. Johnson describes some of the benefits of inclusive businesses. Her studies reveal that venture capitalists are 25% less likely to be successful with their investments when all team members are the same race; however, companies that embrace different backgrounds in their teams will become more engaged and outperform their counterparts by 147%. She notes that inclusive companies are six times as likely to be innovative and anticipate change – they are also twice as likely to meet their financial goals.[162]

Professions will need to work to embrace diversity and inclusion, teams will naturally become more diverse as the Millennial and Generations X and Z mature into the workplace and climb the corporate ladder, but work can always be done to be more inclusive – for instance, for every dollar that a white American holds, black Americans only have five cents, and Hispanic Americans have six cents.[163] As of 2019, women and people of color make up less than 25% and 27%, respectively, of executives and only 5% of CEOs are women.[164]

Asking for a Raise or Advance

After understanding the basics of what factors contribute to a set wage, the history of paying a wage, divisions of labor, now it's time to consider the secondary factors and how they apply in practice. One key secondary factor to consider is the business culture. For this aspect, let's examine Ben Horowitz's *"The Hard Thing About Hard Things: Building a Business When there are No Easy Answers."*

Consider the office culture where one co-worker receives a raise while the others in the office do not. The raise comes from two possible scenarios: the employee asked for the raise, or they were rewarded for a

---

[162] Johnson, 2020.
[163] Johnson, 2020.
[164] Johnson, 2020.

job well done, finalized a major task, or performed highly as part of a yearly review.

When looking at the first scenario, the employee asked for a raise and was awarded extra compensation. Should the other employees find out about the new raise, they might think they were entitled to such a raise. Once other employees begin requesting raises, office politics come into play and creates an unhealthy culture or atmosphere. Therefore, in this scenario, asking for a raise is not recommended for the employee. The manager, in this instance, is also better served by denying such a request.

However, when the second scenario is present, it better serves the employee, the manager, and even the office culture. Next, consider the circumstances around the second scenario – completion of a task, a job well done, or as part of a quarterly or yearly review. Again, office politics arise when considering a raise for a job well done or completing a task. Why should one employee be given a raise while others are completing their tasks as well and at a competent level? At this time, a raise is not warranted unless the entire team or department receives a raise.

This scenario leaves just one optimal time to ask for a raise: a yearly or quarterly performance review. In this instance, the employee and manager are in a confidential environment where the employee may campaign on their efforts, and the manager can offer valuable feedback on the employee's performance. This approach also allows both the employee and manager the ability to justify the raise.

Asking for a Promotion

Much like considering the possibility of a raise, asking for a promotion follows the same lines laid out in Horowitz's "*The Hard Thing About Hard Things.*" Like with a raise request, the best time to ask for a promotion follows a quarterly or yearly review. When asking for a promotion, consider the financial implications that foster sustainable companies. In "*Built to Last,*" Jim Collins and Jerry Porras show that over 90% of CEOs of visionary companies were promoted from within the company. By contrast, over 60% of companies that seek change from hiring outside their own leadership talent fail. [165] By harnessing these statistics that the company is more likely to succeed by promoting within, you are more likely to gain an advantage when asking for a promotion.

Declining a Position

If an offer or promotion has been awarded to the applicant, careful consideration must be given when accepting or declining the offer. My father, for instance, during a forty-year career as a welder and then a "Group Leader," was offered, even recommended by his superiors, to take on the role of a shift supervisor at the place of his employment. He had been promoted up through the ranks to manage groups within his division and managed to set multiple records for keeping production not only on track but ahead of schedule. His position was hourly, and with the state of the economy prior to the 2008 financial crisis and the growth of his company, he knew that he would make higher wages remaining at hourly pay – he made his hourly rate plus overtime due to the growth of the company and demand for their products. However, had he accepted the supervisor position, he would have been placed on a yearly salary – a salary that had the potential to make less than what he would be making working hourly plus the overtime. I don't know that a supervisory position came with any bonuses, but for him, he was comfortable in his role, making adequate income, and maintaining his "normal" hours in lieu of somewhat hectic hours that a supervisor may endure.

Not all promotions or offers are for your own personal benefit. If you have found yourself in a situation that requires declining an offer, treat the correspondence with the utmost respect to the employer. We once had an applicant that was offered a salaried position and then was never to be heard from again. Within industries, many businesses communicate with one another. Failure to communicate with a potential employer could cost you the job at another business because the two companies

---

[165] Collins & Porras, 2005.

mentioned your name in conversation, and your lack of follow-up reflects poorly on your character. In any industry, tactful and respectful communication can go a long way. You are not required to provide any explanation for the rejection, but if you feel comfortable discussing it, you may ease the employer's conscience to some degree.

Section Summary

Along your career path will be milestones and times of difficult conversations that may include your wages, a pay advance, promotion, or even declining a position. Understanding that wages are inevitably built by the hands of others (employees), managers have several key factors to consider when awarding such positions or raises. The difficulty of the position, supply and demand, willingness of employees, and the skill level required of the position contributes to the nonpersonal aspects of a wage. However, personal aspects such as company culture, office politics, and gender will effectively contribute to an individual's salary or an hourly wage. When you consider that women are less likely to negotiate their pay, they may urge them to do so to close the pay gap, whereas male managers or colleagues may campaign for equal pay among their peers. Company culture and office politics can be eliminated in the decision-making process by bringing up a pay raise or promotion during annual or quarterly reviews in private settings and indisputable or arbitrary moments. Sometimes, not all positions or promotions are suited for the individual; however, the candidate is best served in declining such a position in a respectable manner to grow future opportunities that do align with their personal goals.

Chapter 9: Effective Communication

Whether as an employee or a manager, effective communication within a team is highly valued. Effective office communication can be influenced by office culture, managing styles, the work environment – built and perceived – personalities, and office politics, to name a few.

Regarding effective communication Christine Porath's *"Mastering Civility: A Manifesto for the Workplace"* is a valuable work that examines some of the consequences and impacts that negative communication can have on an organization and the health of employees. Porath notes that incivility in the workplace can have life-threatening health problems. During one of her research studies, middle-aged employees with "little to no coworkers support" were more likely to die during the study at an astounding rate of 2.4 times their counterparts.[166]

Porath notes that in financial terms, the American Psychological Association estimates that incivility costs organizations a combined $500 billion per year in the United States alone. Compounding this effect, 550 billion workdays are lost due to stress each year, 60-80% of workplace accidents occur because of stress, 80% of doctor visits are caused by stress – and this all results in 46% higher medical costs than for their non-stressed counterparts.[167]

Diving even deeper, surveys documented in her book indicate that employees who were stressed in the workplace or felt incivility at their place of work, 48% of respondents decreased their efforts, 47% decreased their time spent at work, and 38% of workers decreased the quality of their work. In picking one incident of incivility, 80% of workers lost time worrying about the incident, 63% lost time avoiding the offender, 66% noted a decline in performance, 78% noted a decline in commitment to the organization, 25% of employees admitted to taking frustrations out on customers. Even an astounding 12% of respondents said they had left a job because of uncivil treatment. The cost to turnover

---

[166] Porath, 2016.
[167] Porath, 2016.

due to incivility can total nearly four times the annual salary of high performers. These factors, when compounded, increase costs for a company, build up stress on employees, and can lead to losses of employees and customers.[168]

While the reader now understands some of the consequences – company costs and even loss of life – you may begin to look at some of the factors that not only cause incivility but ways to cultivate effective communication in its place. Using aspects such as how an office or workplace is constructed, arrangement of teams, and finally, Porath's methods for cultivating civility, a path towards more effective communication can begin to take shape. While these methods are not exhaustive by any means, it is my hope that they begin to outline the framework for offices and workplaces to tailor concepts to fit their place of business specifically.

A Lesson in Civility

Circling back to Porath's "*Mastering Civility*," it is worth noting she created a Civility Test. Using some of the concepts above, consider your own behavior within the work setting and take her "Are you Civil?" test. The results will vary for everyone, but she emphasizes that this exam is more for noticing blind spots and areas upon which we can all improve. Here are her steps for fostering your own civility:

1. Ask for focused feedback on your best and worst behaviors. This approach asks readers to survey ten to fifteen colleagues regarding your behavior. Collect the feedback and seek out common themes – these will be your attributes and areas to build upon.

---

[168] Porath, 2016.

2. Work with a coach. Coaches can help you find blind spots among colleagues and ourselves, as well as identify ways of mending weaknesses and fostering strengths.

3. Conduct a team tune-up. Where a team environment is present, schedule a sit-down to discuss areas where the team could improve or where respect may not be shown directly. You can also create your own team – including friends, colleagues, and coaches – to tune up behavioral areas.

4. Get 360 feedback. 360 feedback can come from direct reports from teammates, supervisors, colleagues – really anyone who can contribute to the "360-degree" evaluation.

5. Teach yourself how to read emotions. The ability to read others' emotions can always be refined. Porath notes her go-to list for how to become better at reading emotions.

6. Make time for reflection. Take time to reflect on concepts learned, areas improved, and track progress.

7. Take care of yourself. Porath suggests that you get plenty of exercise, eat nutritional meals, and find stress management techniques to improve your overall wellbeing, which will help increase your civility.[169]

Built Environment, Obstacle, or Opening

The first component of effective communication depends on the inanimate objects – the built environment. The layout of an office greatly impacts the way coworkers communicate with one another. Considering different personality types, as Susan Cain discusses in *"Quiet: The*

---

[169] Porath, 2016.

Power of Introverts in a World that Can't Stop Talking," creative types, most often associated with introverts, typically operate better in solitude. This fact is further evidenced in a study Cain reviews in detail in which students and their cooperation levels are measured while working in pods or small clusters. This environment is not always the best way to work; in fact, Cain indicates that over seventy percent of corporate employees work in open office layouts – meaning that over 70% of employees working in an office are not as productive as they could be simply due to the layout of their workspace.[170]

To add additional evidence to the theory that the design of a workplace impacts productivity, look toward "*The Culture Code*" by Daniel Coyle. He indicates that it may not entirely be the design of the space that influences communication - but the distance between the desks themselves. Adding another layer to the built environment, vertical separation causes even further breakdown in communication, whereas horizontal distances seem to impact communication less. Coyle goes on to describe the mechanisms behind the "Allen Curve," a rule in which those closer in proximity encourage connection and interaction. [171]

"*The Culture Code*" should be referenced again when looking at effective communication within teams. In a study of interaction patterns within groups, Coyle notes the following as key elements of successful teams. Teams worked and communicated best while in close physical proximity to one another; an appropriate amount of eye contact and physical touches such as handshakes enhance the nonverbal factors of communication. All team members speak to one another with few interruptions in short exchanges. There are, ideally, lots of questions, active listening, and laughter.

---

[170] Cain, 2013.
[171] Coyle, 2018.

The Personality of Guppies

Scientists once studied freshwater guppies to understand how environmental factors accompanied by inherited traits impacted the personalities of guppies. In their initial experiments, the guppies were placed in a pool with a population of pike – natural predators of guppies – and witnessed cautious, introverted personality traits exhibited by the guppies. Slowly over time, the pike was removed, and the scientists noted a simultaneous shift in the personality of the guppies – they were slowly becoming more extroverted and venturing further from safe locations within the pool. Eventually, all pike had vanished from the experiment pool. The guppies had then evolved over generations into extroverted, careless specimens wandering far and wide from their safe zones. Scientists then reintroduced pike to the environment, and the extroverted guppies were subsequently vanquished from the pool by hungry predators. The remaining guppies still exhibited introverted traits that inherently told them not to venture far from safe locations. What scientists concluded was that the personalities of the guppies shifted as the fear of predators decreased; in addition, the extroverted guppies led other guppies, in their own form of communication, to exhibit these same characteristics, and even impacted personalities of future generations, which led to their eventual demise.[172]

I bring this up because the next contributing factor in effective communication comes from understanding your teams' personality types. Here, Cain dissects how the current marketplace consists of extroverted personality types, one may also wonder if these extroverted personality types and their proclivity for finding enjoyment in gambling may have led to the financial crisis of 2008. At any rate, different types of leaders work better with different types of employees. Cain notes that introverted leaders are better at working with, or better yet – coaching employees who are self-starters and take the initiative. Extroverted

---

[172] Cain, 2013.

131

leaders obtain better results when working with passive, task-focused employees.[173]

Brendan Kane's *"One Million Followers"* discusses the benefits of creating messages for the masses and how they resonate among six different personality types. Your team might consist of the following personalities:

1. Thinkers (25%) perceive the world through thoughts; logic is their currency.

2. Persisters perceive the world through opinions; value is their currency.

3. Harmonizers (30%) perceive the world through emotions; compassion is their currency.

4. Imaginers perceive the world through inactions; imagination is their currency.

5. Rebels (20%) perceive the world through reactions; humor is their currency.

6. Promoters perceive the world through actions; charm is their currency.[174]

Both Coyle's *"The Culture Code"* and Horowitz's *"What You Do is Who You Are"* prove instructive for office politics and office culture. Both authors take a fascinating look into what office culture truly is and what it takes to influence a positive work environment. Consider, for instance,

---

[173] Cain, 2013.
[174] Kane, 2018.

Coyle's "Ideas for Action" chapter for concepts that can be implemented within teams to foster not only a healthy culture but effective communication. His action items are to over-communicate that you are listening, spotlight your own ability to fail early on, embrace the messenger, preview future relationships, use thank you profusely, be painstaking in your hiring processes, create safe environments, ensure everyone has a voice, capitalize on threshold moments, embrace fun, and avoid what he calls "sandwich feedback."[175]

Business and Office Culture

How valuable is a healthy business culture? Coyle cites a staggering statistic that businesses can increase their income by, on average, an estimated 765% over ten years.[176]

In looking at office culture, Horowitz defines it as an alignment of personality and strategy, based on action and not words, with an openness to outside talent; a place that seeks coaching – not directing – and encourages empowerment. Office cultures are often expressed when we're not there to monitor them, and our values and principles are translated among our coworkers and employees. According to Horowitz, once employees absorb an office culture, it will manifest itself everywhere within the company; therefore, always be attentive to how you set an example.[177]

Combining office culture and personality, Gladwell's concept of the "Diffusion Model" proves instructive. Employees and members of teams might fall into one of four of Gladwell's categories: innovators, early adopters, late adopters, and the laggards. Placing personnel in certain roles within an office or organization can either assist or handicap effective communication within a team. Gladwell goes on to describe the

---

[175] Coyle, 2018.
[176] Coyle, 2018.
[177] Horowitz, 2019.

"Rule of 150," where optimal performance in society is limited to a population of one hundred fifty individuals. Within this model, each teammate and the team operates with a "channel capacity," or the amount of information that can be processed at one time. [178]

Organizational Health and Communication

Thus far, this chapter has looked at the physical and built environment's impacts on effective communication, elements of successful teams, team personalities, and how the diffusion model and channel capacity spread office culture, politics, and civility. Let's now turn our attention to what Patrick Lencioni calls organizational health in his book, *"The Advantage: Why Organizational Health Trumps Everything Else in Business."* To understand this concept, Lencioni argues that organizational health can be simplified to two types of businesses – Smart Businesses and Healthy Businesses.[179]

The first type, Smart Business, are those businesses that are wonderful at making analytical and savvy decisions, stressing strategy, and noting the importance of finances and marketing. They are extremely adept at being leaders in their pragmatic approach to business, but sometimes corner themselves into being inept at making the change due to thinking, "this is the way we have always done it," and believing too much in their own experience to allow for new ideas and innovation which causes a decline in growth. Their inability to learn returns these businesses to mediocre status or, even worse, decreases sales and eventual closure. [180]

The second type, Healthy Businesses, has minimal politics, carries high employee and office morale, and maintains low turnover. These healthy businesses gain knowledge over time which helps mitigate risk and failures as the company grows and matures. Unhealthy organizations

---

[178] Gladwell, 2000.
[179] Lencioni, 2012.
[180] Lencioni, 2012.

simply have high turnover, low morale caused by nonconstructive conflict, and toxic office politics.[181]

Lencioni provides a framework to build organizational health by outlining four disciplines that need to be fostered to set the path to healthier businesses. They are:

DISCIPLINE 1: Build a cohesive leadership team.

DISCIPLINE 2: Create clarity.

DISCIPLINE 3: Over-communicate clarity.

DISCIPLINE 4: Reinforce clarity.[182]

To break these disciplines down one by one, first look at Lencioni's two modes of communication: advocacy and inquiry. The first is the point of advocacy – this communication type advocates for a point of view or a stance on an item; the second point of inquiry is where people ask questions for clarity on the advocacy comments. [183]

So now that we know what organizational health is and the two modes of communication, we look at the initial discipline: building cohesive leadership teams. The first takeaway put forth by Lencioni is that teams must be able to build trust. Vulnerable trust allows employees and managers to communicate openly and honestly in comfortable, nonthreatening environments. He also notes that profiling uncovers

---

[181] Lencioni, 2012.
[182] Lencioni, 2012.
[183] Lencioni, 2012.

neutral information regarding each of the key players on the team; remember the personality traits from earlier chapters? Take everyone's personality types and introduce these into the discussion. The second take-away: mastering conflict. Healthy conflict allows for open debate and discussion without politics, hostility, or judgment. The third take-away behavior consists of achieving commitment, and Lencioni notes: "If people don't weigh in, they won't buy in." Each member and each team should make specific agreements or tasks for each discussion. This approach leads to the fourth behavior: embracing accountability. Address one another to keep employees accountable instead of going to their, or your, superiors first. This tactic allows you to open a one-on-one dialogue and address any conflict or issues readily. Behavior number five: focus on the results. These results should be contributing to the goals that are set and shared across the team. By mastering these five behaviors, a cohesive leadership team can evolve and grow. [184]

The second discipline focuses on creating clarity. Lencioni posits that six critical questions and their answers can help to provide the crucial clarity to define an organization's health. Here are his six critical questions:

1. Why do we exist?
   Consider your core purpose and how you create a better world and community. Be aspirational and idealistic in your answers.

2. How do we behave?
   What are your values in terms of core values and aspirational values? Core values should be limited to one or two that lie at the heart of your company. The aspirational values are those you hold as worthy of striving toward.

3. What do we do?
   This is much like a mission statement – but much simpler. Keep it to one sentence, with simple, easy definitions.

---

[184] Lencioni, 2012.

4. How will we succeed?
   This question helps you define your strategy and how to implement it.

5. What is important right now?
   "If everything is important, then nothing is important." Prioritize items listed within your strategy and implement them first.

6. Who must do what?
   One of the most important questions considers who does what and when. Once a strategy is developed, components are prioritized, and tasks are delegated to each team member to begin the implementation in an organized manner. [185]

Finally, disciplines three and four hold many similarities. Over-communicate the clarity developed in discipline number two, and then reinforce the clarity of the new organizational health.

Social Chemistry of Effective Communication

When evaluating a new place of employment or reviewing your own workplace, finding answers to the above-mentioned questions, and gaining open, cooperative feedback and answers may be difficult. Marissa King's *"Social Chemistry"* presents the concept of "Psychological Safety" and its effects on a business. She cites a study in which 85% of respondents noted that they were afraid to speak up due to being judged or negatively seen by their peers or employers. She also cites a two-year study performed by Google entitled "Project Aristotle," which sought a formula for creating the best team; instead, it identified

---

[185] Lencioni, 2012.

five key principles to developing a cohesive and effective team. Instead of focusing on introverts versus extroverts, personality types, or other factors, they discovered the following as the key principles: employees sought dependability, employees needed structure; clarity around goals and roles was paramount; employees wanted to find meaning in their work and wanted to hold the idea that the work the team was doing mattered. [186]

King's statistics show that only 30% of respondents in her studies felt safe to speak up and that these numbers can be improved. She notes that one of the most effective ways to foster psychological safety within teams is to end the blame game. Instead of focusing on who is to blame, spend energy on fixing any issues and overcoming obstacles. One of her concluding statements on psychological safety shows the difference between trust and psychological safety: trust is a long-term investment made in a one-on-one relationship and focuses on the future. Psychological safety provides immediate results and impacts the team or group as a whole. [187]

Psychological safety will set the tone for effective office communication and should be greatly considered when accepting or rejecting a job offer, promotion, or raise. When evaluated from the outside, psychological safety and organizational health will provide you with a strong understanding of how your future career would take shape within the place of business. Not only would your career be shaped, but your health and overall happiness and satisfaction depend on evaluating these criteria when weighing your decisions.

---

[186] King, 2021.
[187] King, 2021.

Section Summary

Effective communication is one of the most important ways of building your career. Instead of being perceived as rude, demanding, or incompatible with others – focus on building rapport within your resume and portfolio, networking, interviewing, job negotiations, and years on the job that constructs a positive atmosphere for all parties. Unknowingly, your built environment may be hindering your ability to access those that may hire you, promote you within the company, or even foster a successful team. If a company has these built obstacles, find ways to work around them to increase your own communication with those you need to speak with. Consider the different personalities you will encounter on your career path. When we understand that people perform in concert with their personality, their teammates realize that they are "hard-wired" instead of creating fault or a biased perspective of them. These communication methods contribute to the office culture. Most people think office culture is related to incentives or perks such as a bar in the break room or a pool table in the lounge, but instead, it is how we interact with one another and at what level of efficacy.

The culture garnered within companies leads to smart or healthy businesses. Smart businesses may lead to feelings of monotony within your day-to-day roles, whereas healthy businesses will find ways to encourage you to grow and innovate. These healthy businesses also lead to psychological safety where employees feel safe to contribute to the company's overall mission. A healthy business produces healthy employees.

Chapter 10: The When Factor

Most of the concepts covered above outline the who, what, and how to proceed through certain aspects of an individual's professional career. However, one often little-discussed factor, the when factor, can have a greater impact than most realize. Consider Daniel H. Pink's "*When: The Scientific Secrets of Perfect Timing,*" which notes a startling study reflecting twenty years of research. The study followed recently graduated white men, a category the author notes is least impacted by gender or racial biases over twenty years beginning in the late 1980s. The findings were stark and revealed that those who graduated when the economy was prosperous and unemployment rates were low earned, on average, $100,000 more over a span of twenty years than did their peers who graduated in low-performing economies with high unemployment. Not only did the state of the economy impact their earnings, but it also showed that those who graduated in poor economic conditions also stayed at their jobs longer – not happily, but with mismatched skills and talents that were then spent at a job they felt stuck at. Recent survey results, Pink notes, show that recent graduates (those who graduated in the year 2010-2011) had nearly double the negative effects than researchers had previously found in their studies performed in the 1980s. The takeaway is that those who graduated during the Great Recession continued to struggle professionally and financially.[188]

In "*Can't Even: How Millennials Became the Burnout Generation,*" Anne Helen Petersen notes more stark statistics: the unemployment rate doubled from five to ten percent between 2007 to 2009, which resulted in a loss of 8.6 million jobs. For young professionals of this era, those aged 16-24, the residual effects were felt even harder: between November 2007 and April 2010 the unemployment rate rose drastically from 10.8% to 19.5% - resulting in the young professionals entering the worst hiring market in 80 years. [189]

---

[188] Pink, 2019.
[189] Petersen, 2021.

From this data, we see those outside forces such as the stock market, economy, and unemployment rates can have an unfair impact on a future employee; it all depends on when a graduate, or someone seeking a new career path, begins their job search. Considerations should be given to the when factor. When is the right time to choose to change positions? How will the market be prepared for my degree following graduation? Will that have any impact on the field of study? When should I retire?

Workflow, Happiness, and Meaning

Another consideration for those seeking career change is the aspect of happiness at work. Mihaly Csikszentmihalyi has spent a career writing about the aspects he calls "flow." In his book "*Good Business: Leadership, Flow, and the Making of Meaning*," Csikszentmihalyi states that there are two pillars to happiness: differentiation and integration. When individuals realize that they are unique and responsible for their own happiness and well-being, with freedom of choice and autonomy, they practice differentiation. Integration is how to take our individual strengths and skills that differentiate us from others and combine them with those of others to integrate into an efficient, highly functional organization or team. [190]

"Flow" consists of eight factors when felt at work. The first factor comes from having clear goals. Employees will know what is expected of them, what is within their control and sphere of influence. They can exercise their autonomy in every step towards a clear, concise goal. However, the state of flow is achieved within the journey and not necessarily the destination. In a good flow state, employees find themselves entrenched in their work and enjoying the task at hand. The second factor focuses on instant feedback so that individuals can apply their skills working through a task and gain immediate responses to the efficacy of the work within the task.

---

[190] Csikszentmihalyi, 2004.

Also important: striking a balance between challenge and opportunity. The work itself must be challenging enough to keep the employee motivated and focused while balancing these challenges with an appropriate amount of skill. Skills should be ever-growing. As the skillset expands, challenges may then become more complex. As this balance and constant one-upping occur, the fourth factor arises: the deepening of concentration. Individuals note that when they enter a flow state, tasks can seem effortless. If so, they can approach the fifth factor: control. People in flow feel a sense of control over the task, but at the same time, their passionate work tends to take over. They enter a state of, as Csikszentmihalyi says, ecstasy (which he cites as originating from the Latin meaning of "to be aside from" leading them to be at the behest of the work and task itself). This aspect continues the sixth factor: doing the task simply for the sake of doing it.

While all of these factors are in action, the seventh factor takes over: all sense of time seems altered. Workers note that they feel as though time either flies by or stands still while their task consumes and overtakes them. The eighth and final component is the loss of ego: the stage in which no person completing the work does it for themselves but simply does it for the journey, the sense of accomplishment, and to achieve the harmonious balance of challenge and skill. [191]

Entering flow at work greatly increases productivity and efficiency within a business. As noted in previous chapters, those working in healthy, civil, and productive offices tend to be happier and better at their professions. Flow, or the ability to find happiness while performing the task at hand, offers something more than mere profits. What happens when one finds their flow state? Csikszentmihalyi describes two different types of rewards that a person can feel: autotelic and exotelic. Autotelic, translated from Latin to mean "self-goal," are rewards that people find happiness and accomplishment in the work itself. By contrast, exotelic rewards are outside through means of raises, promotions, or bonuses that provide minimal or momentary happiness

---

[191] Csikszentmihalyi, 2004.

and quickly fade. Therefore, in weighing the suitable fit of your current position, or one you are about to accept or consider, you should seriously consider the intrinsic rewards of achieving flow for your autotelic reward. Can you focus on work, or are you interrupted often, which disrupts the ability to reach flow? Are your challenges and skillsets in balance or organized in such a way to increase both equally for continued growth? [192]

Flowing with Challenge, Skilled at Happiness

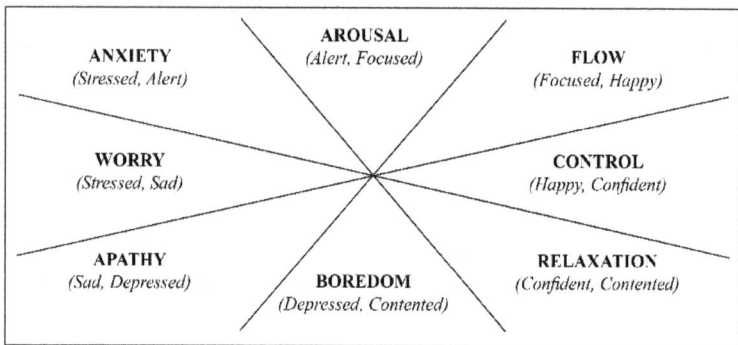

ANXIETY (Stressed, Alert)	AROUSAL (Alert, Focused)	FLOW (Focused, Happy)
WORRY (Stressed, Sad)		CONTROL (Happy, Confident)
APATHY (Sad, Depressed)	BOREDOM (Depressed, Contented)	RELAXATION (Confident, Contented)

Figure 1: "Figure 2: The Map of Everyday Experience" from Good Business: Leadership Flow, and the Making of Meaning by Mihaly Csikszentmihalyi, copyright © 2003 by Mihaly Csikszentmihalyi. Used by permission of Viking Books, an imprint of Penguin Publishing Group, a Division of Penguin Random House LLC. All rights reserved.

To further the effects of flow on one's own happiness at work, consider the simple conclusion reached by Csikszentmihalyi, where he draws parallels between skills and challenges. Initially, we look to tasks that offer low challenges and require low skills. This results in both low boredom and low anxiety. This type of work could be termed as busy work. As the matrix increases in challenge without advancing in skill, workers often feel low boredom yet high anxiety. Vice versa, where the

---

[192] Csikszentmihalyi, 2004.

146

work requires high skills yet offers no challenge, workers increase in boredom and less so on anxiety. However, when the skills and challenges both increase, a state of flow can be embraced. [193]

Diving deeper, Csikszentmihalyi's research revealed that when employees performed tasks that lacked both complexity and skill, individuals claimed to feel apathy and a sense of depression and sadness. When slightly more challenge or complexity is added, these individuals then started to feel a sense of worry in which they were both sad and stressed. When workers were overwhelmed with complexity and lacked the necessary skillset, they felt anxiety and increased stress. [194]

Where tasks are simple and lacked complexity yet required more skill, employees felt bored and remained depressed while still being content with the work. Increasing the complexity of the task then raised their feelings of arousal, alertness, and focus. They were exercising more of their skills while working on these more difficult challenges. In situations that require high skillsets but rank low on complexity, workers would feel relaxed, confident, and content to be doing the work. [195]

When workers utilize most of their skillsets and slightly increase the complexity, employees then gained control of their work and felt both happy and content at the task. When complexity and challenges increase to a level that matches a high skillset, employees finally enter their state of flow – they are focused, happy, utilizing the maximum of their resources, and accomplishing detailed tasks. [196]

How often do you enter your state of flow? In reaching a flow state, you will become happier and exercise more civility and control within the workplace. Being a more amiable part of the team helps increase the efficacy of the team itself as well as the organization in its entirety. If you cannot reach your own flow state, perhaps evaluating the current

---

[193] Csikszentmihalyi, 2004.
[194] Csikszentmihalyi, 2004.
[195] Csikszentmihalyi, 2004.
[196] Csikszentmihalyi, 2004.

circumstances to find ways of reaching flow are in order, or you may begin to look elsewhere for other opportunities.

Section Summary

Undoubtedly, Gen-X, Gen-Z, and Millennials will begin their careers far behind others economically. Most individuals in the workforce innately realize this and seek positions that provide meaning, purpose, and happiness instead of financial incentives. When a raise or promotion is not readily available or even distantly visible, employees will begin to look elsewhere within the company to find fulfillment. If that fulfillment cannot be found within the company, employees will begin to look elsewhere for meaning and purpose.

To retain individuals, businesses should look at ways of building flow states in their work environments. Job applicants should seek out opportunities to achieve their own flow states, if not, you may be signing up for a job that offers very little fulfillment and leads to high turnover rates, and ultimately, you are looking for a new job. Seek areas in which your skills are challenged in balance with the complexity of the tasks you will be performing to find your own flow states at work.

Chapter 11: Planning for Retirement and Beyond

A Father's Lesson

Growing up, my parents let my sister and I join our local 4-H chapter: Stanberry Lucky Clover 4-H. I was only eight years old when I signed up, and there wasn't much in the way of options for me to participate. One of the few options was "Beef Cattle." We didn't own any livestock at the time, but my parents signed me up, and we went and bought a small, mixed-breed heifer for my sister and me to raise. (We had a small 10-acre pasture to accommodate this, I don't recommend going out and buying a cow on a whim). As part of the Beef Cattle program, the member would raise the calf on their own, train it to lead – some cows were led around like it was a pet dog – and then show the heifer or steer in the county fair. The first calf we purchased on Valentine's Day lovingly became known as Valentine. My sister and I worked with her every day, and she became one of our pets. I was able to show her the following summer at the county fair – I was the only little guy in the arena. I was leading this calf as a first grader among high schoolers. It was a bit strange seeing a little kid with these bigger kids – so the following year, they invented the pee-wee class. I was the only one in the division that year, so I won.

Some months later, my father told us it was time to sell Valentine so we could purchase our next show calf. My sister and I were sad that we had to give up our pet, but we were learning responsibility, ownership, and the ways of a working farm – one show calf at a time. When we sold her, my father told me that I had to split the money with my sister since she helped raise Valentine. He also took out the cost of the feed to raise the calf and the original money invested to purchase her. My sister and I had our first take-home pay: $65 each. That's a lot of money for an eight-year-old! We then counted our dollar bills and gave them back to my father, so he could purchase another calf for both my sister and I. (Disclaimer, you cannot buy an entire cow for $65, my father just let us believe this so we would understand the concept of expenses, bills, and investments).

The cycle continued for a few more years, and by the time I was twelve years old, I was purchasing my own cattle – at market rate, not the family discount rate. I would grab the Sunday classified from the newspaper, sprawl out on the living room floor, and flip directly to the "Farm and Garden" section to see what ads were listed for cattle. What my father didn't realize was that he was training a little thrifty mastermind who would nickel and dime a deal to make more profit. I would read the rest of the newspaper for other "cow" related articles. Then, in 2003, the first case of Mad Cow Disease was found in the United States. The market tumbled. At that time, Brazil was one of the largest competitors for beef cattle exports, second only behind the United States – how did I know to look for this at the age of 12 or 13?! When Mad Cow Disease was discovered, other countries stopped all imports of the infected country's livestock, which meant a surplus was growing within the States. This is good for everyday people at the grocery store. Simple supply and demand would dictate that too many cattle meant they were being sold at lower prices, leading to lower prices for hamburgers, steaks, and the like.

I then scoured the classifieds even harder, trying to find the best deals. There was a stocker (a farmer who buys bulk numbers of cattle at lower prices, then sells them in smaller quantities at higher prices) who always had these ad hoc herds put together with some of the weirdest looking cows. (He at one point had a full-blooded Brahma bull that looked like a Zebu – Google it). From this stocker, I purchased a scrawny, gray steer with a white face with hopes of raising and fattening him, then later selling him for a profit. Life had different plans for the poor soul, though, as happens from time to time. One day, the calf drank from the pond and got stuck in the mud while we were away. He wasn't strong enough to pull himself out and eventually perished along the pond bank. My investment had been lost.

My father knew that I hadn't done anything wrong in the investment, I hadn't squandered any money, the poor calf, unfortunately, passed away, and there wasn't anything we could do about it. My father, seeing my despair, said he would make me a deal – he would trade my calf with a cow/calf pair that he had. I agreed. The cow went on to produce more calves throughout the years that we raised and sold. Combining this with my summer job income that I had accumulated throughout high school, I purchased two completely paid-off vehicles. I walked to my first day of college with a savings account of nearly $13,000.

That small investment in Valentine allowed me to focus on my five-year master's degree without working through the school year, and I accumulated additional funds working during the summers. I was financially secure to enjoy my college years, having rent and bills paid through my cattle investments and saving over time. What my father instilled in me from age eight was that if I invested my funds and waited patiently, the return would come back eventually. While I couldn't enjoy the fruits of my labor right away, patience allowed me to live focused solely on my studies throughout my entire college career. The savings account dried up quickly after college, though – being a college student and frequenting college bars derailed a few saving milestones.

I share this life lesson for many reasons. The first is that even at an early age, I was investing. I was reading articles and learning about the industry and markets. I prioritized my spending and maximized my profits. I learned the true value of something rather than the cost of something. The more time you can invest in something and let it grow on its own, the better the investment outcome and higher rewards. Politics and world events shape the markets, education provides a framework, and a patient mindset allows investments to mature – all of which are necessary when discussing any aspect of your finances. (Side note, in 2014, the Dakotas, Wyoming, Montana, and central Canadian provinces had one of the worst winters on record, causing several thousand cattle to perish due to inclement weather and farmers unable to tend to them. This led to the smallest cattle herd in the United States since 1965. Our cattle in Missouri were ready for sale in a high-demand market – and in 2015, I was able to put a down payment on a Cadillac with the profits of that one year alone).

Timing Your Retirement

When is the right time to begin planning for retirement or your eventual transition out of the professional field? *"Built to Last"* authors Collins and Porras suggest that truly visionary companies begin planning very early on – not just with a five-year plan, but what does the transition look like ten, twenty, even fifty years down the road? They recommend three questions to ask yourself: what are your top three opportunities to accomplish? What are your top three things to stop doing? Finally, what are your top three support mechanisms? Asking yourself these three questions yearly, every five years or even every ten can put your retirement and transition into a planned perspective. [197]

The Importance of Retirement Plans

Petersen's *"Can't Even: How Millennials Became the Burnout Generation"* describes a pension plan in a simplified definition. A pension plan is a mechanism for employees to contribute a portion of their earnings to an account. This account is utilized during their retirement as a means of recompense for their years of service to the company. In 1980, of all private-sector employees, 46% were covered by a pension plan compared to only 16% in 2019. A 2012 study revealed that 53% of private-sector employees had access to contribution plans such as 401K or IRAs. Petersen contests that these plans are considered access plans versus participation plans – meaning employees struggle to contribute to these plans consistently. This trend is echoed in the same 2012 study where only 38% of the 53% enrolled in the contribution plans. [198]

Programs such as Social Security began in the United States as a way to supplement retirees' income and keep the elderly from living in poverty. Author Paul Taylor, a researcher with the Pew Research Center, cites in

---

[197] Collins & Porras, 2005.
[198] Petersen, 2021.

his book, "*The Next America: Boomers, Millennials, and the Looming Generational Showdown*," that when Social Security began, on average, 42 contributors paid for one retiree drawing benefits. However, by 2035, that number will drop to an astounding two to one. By the time all Boomers retire, nearly half of the government budget will go to programs such as Medicare, Social Security, and the non-child portion of Medicaid. This is reflected in further studies in which a fifty-year span revealed that the United States government went from paying $3 on general expenses such as education, roads, and infrastructure for every $1 spent on entitlements such as Social Security and Medicare; however, the ratio will reverse course by 2035 and the government will spend $5 on entitlements for every $1 spent elsewhere. [199]

Taylor's research of a United States survey in which participants were asked if they felt confident that they would have an adequate standard of living in old age, 24% of respondents were "very" while 39% were "somewhat" confident. [200] However, the average lifespan of a baby born in the United States today is 78.7 years and goes up on average, one year for every six. By 2050, it is estimated that the United States will have approximately one-half million people living to see age 100. [201] This leads to a dependency ratio (working-age adults supporting nonworking individuals – including youth and the elderly), which will climb from 1:19 in 2010 to 1:36 by 2050. [202]

The dependency ratio, average lifespan, and amounts spent on entitlements will lead every working adult to a need to earn a wage to support two individuals. Statistics provided by Taylor reflect that this scenario is beginning to play out as the labor force within the United States for those 65 and older grew from 10.8% in 1985 to 18.5% in 2012. Today's employees are required to stay in the workforce longer, for less pay, and need to draw upon private investments into IRAs and 401K

---

[199] Taylor, 2014.
[200] Taylor, 2014.
[201] Taylor, 2014.
[202] Taylor, 2014.

programs so that they can support their lifestyles – as well as at least one Boomer. [203]

Some experts note that a large transfer of wealth will be inevitable with the passing of the Boomer generation. Taylor's statistics note that the ratio of wealth versus income, as of 2011, had grown for Boomers to a staggering 26x the wealth of younger households, which was up from 10x in the mid-1980s. However, as we have learned in the previous paragraphs, this accumulated wealth of the Boomer generation will be spent on Medicare and Medicaid as their generation ages. All the while, they will also be absorbing benefits from Social Security, leaving the Millennial, Gen-X, and Gen-Z workforce to pay for everything. [204]

Retirement Mechanisms

In short, young professionals today begin their careers at a significant disadvantage compared to previous generations; however, steps may be taken early within their careers to counter the negative hiring markets, recessions, and challenges of other debts (such as credit cards and student loans, to name a few). Erin Lowry's *"Broke Millennial Takes on Investing: A Beginner's Guide to Leveling Up Your Money"* recommends beginning saving for retirement early. She outlines three important items that all young professionals should know.

The first item is to become familiar with compound interest, which in essence allows one to make interest from interest. [205] The concept behind compound interest is that an individual makes an initial investment, for simplicity's sake, say $100 through the first year of the investment, may average eight percent growth leading to $8 being gained through interest and resulting in a balance of $108 for allowing the funds to remain in the market. The $108 again makes a return of 8% interest the following year, resulting in a gain of $8.64. After two years, averaging 8% return on

---

[203] Taylor, 2014.
[204] Taylor, 2014.
[205] Lowry, 2019.

investments, one would have $116.64, having only invested $100. While $16.64 may not seem like much, continue this trend for 30 years, and you would have $1,007 from simply investing $100 at an average rate of return of 8% compounded annually – and that was a one-time contribution.

The advice leads to the second item that Lowry notes: time is on your side. Beginning your retirement account as early as possible allows you to harness the power of compound interest and further your returns. Whether a 401K or IRA, the retirement account serves the purpose of the third item that she notes: investing in a retirement account guards against inflation because your investments are diversified and will not lose value over time. Consider the difference between buying an item in 1930 versus the cost to purchase it in 2030 – that is inflation wreaking havoc on the purchasing power of a single dollar. [206]

Now equipped with the statistics from above and Lowry's three key points, the next step is to learn common investing terms. Lowry outlines the following key terms to know:

1. Investing: putting your money to work for you.

2. Asset Class: grouping of similar investments.

3. Portfolio: the overall picture of all your investments.

4. Public or Publicly Traded Companies: you are able to purchase stock in the company. Stock is usually sold to the public when the company is trying to raise substantial sums of money for growth opportunities or pay down existing debts.

5. Equity or Stock: a piece of the company.

---

[206] Lowry, 2019.

6. Shares: what stock are divided into.

7. Shareholder/Stockholder: someone who owns stock in a company at a rate of x-x-number of shares.

8. Securities: holdings of equity (stocks) or debts (bonds).

9. Bonds: a portion of the government's debt. The government sells bonds to finance projects such as infrastructure or buildings. These bonds consist of your money, and over time, the government slowly repays the bond amount.

10. Maturity: when a debt comes full-term.

11. Fixed-Income: bonds are set payments.

12. Cash/Cash Equivalent: liquid assets are easily accessible. Cash is well, cash, such as a savings account where there are no fees associated with the money being held. CDs are cash-equivalent funds where money is invested in a fund for a certain period of time and then is relinquished back to the investor with a small percentage of interest.

13. Asset Allocation: where all of the investments go.

14. Diversification: spreading investments in several funds to average out losses and gains for a steady growth opportunity.

15. Sectors: industries.

16. Time Horizon: how soon do you plan to retire or need the funds available?

17. Risk Tolerance: the gut feeling you get when losing money. Can you risk losing it all, or would you prefer to have safer investments at a lower rate of gain?

18. Brokerage Account: where money is deposited to be invested.

19. Portfolio Manager: a fiduciary (someone ethically obligated to serve and invest in your best interest) who manages your investments.

20. Return on Investment (ROI): the return on something expended.

21. Mutual Fund: pooling money together from different investors.

22. Exchange Trade Fund (ETF): funds traded instantaneously during trading hours.

23. Dividend: if a company is profitable during a quarter or a year, the company will pay shareholders dividends or a portion of the profits.

24. Dividend Investment Program (DIP): a passive way of investing your returns.[207]

While this list is not exhaustive by any means, it can provide a basic understanding of some of the terms being used in the investing world. Utilizing the three concepts above, the knowledge of some key terms, and the understanding that time is of the essence when beginning a retirement fund are all vital. However, Lowry goes on to guide her readers through some additional steps to take when starting your investments. Here they are:

---

[207] Lowry, 2019.

1. Investing is not just for wealthy people, and the earlier you start, the better off the investment will be. Begin by determining your own personal financial goals: what would you like to achieve in the short- and long term?

2. The next step is to master your cash flow. Understanding your assets and liabilities, when money is coming in, and what money is going out will allow you to prioritize your budget strategically. Ensure that a portion of your income is dedicated to a savings account so that it can be set aside for an emergency fund. The ideal range is to have somewhere between three and six months of expenses saved in your savings account. Holding the money in a savings account allows for easy, no penalty fee access in times of dire need.

3. Next, consider any larger upcoming expenses: new tires for the car, car insurance, vehicle registration, you name it. With these expenses accounted for, they can be included within the budget and saved over several months instead of an upfront cost when the expense is due.

4. Finally, Lowry's last tips include educating yourself about the stock market, investing in retirement funds, especially if your company provides a matching percentage, and paying off any consumer debt. (Consumer debt is anything other than a mortgage or student loan, including credit cards, personal loans, etc.). These debts often carry high interest rates, which cost hundreds if not thousands of dollars during the repayment period. When purchasing anything on a credit card or using consumer debt – just remember, the expense will consume you.

Section Summary

It may seem odd to discuss retirement when first starting your career, but it is critical to make the most of your investments by starting the process early. When considering employment packages presented during job interviews or when signing up for benefits during your initial week at work, understanding some of the definitions and their implications on your financial outlook in retirement will set you up to prosper and feel comfortable entering your retirement years. Younger generations will support more than themselves and their children in the future, but Boomers will greatly depend on the financial wellbeing of Gen-X, Gen-Z, and Millennials to help support them.

Chapter 12: Synopsis

Closing Thoughts

Throughout this handbook, important aspects aside from the typical aspects of job searching and career advancement have been discussed. While it is important to focus on your resume, portfolio, and interview skills – it is also vital to consider where you apply for a new position, how your current career trajectory is progressing, and the company that surrounds you. Our final set of statistics to present comes from Jacob Morgan's *"The Employee Experience Advantage: How to Win the War for Talent by Giving Employees the Workspaces They Want, The Tools They Need, and a Culture They Can Celebrate."* Morgan helps describe nine different types of organizations that you may encounter in your job search. To understand his definitions of each, we'll first need to look at three areas of concentration in developing environments: technological, physical, and cultural. Echoing sentiments from the *Effective Communication* section, Morgan notes that the physical environment accounts for 30% of an employee's experience. Office or environmental factors to consider should look at whether or not the company allows you to bring in friends or visitors. The importance of this factor is that companies who are pleased to bring in outsiders are comfortable allowing others to judge their workspaces – if they limit visitors or family members to a certain part of the office, chances are they are not comfortable exposing the environment in which they house their employees. Another factor to consider is the opportunity for flexibility – with the COVID-19 pandemic, more and more of the workforce is moving online and working remotely. Giving employees the agency with where and when they work will provide for a more hospitable work experience. Another factor is to ensure that the company's values are present and exhibited within the work environment. Places of business that truly represent their mission and values will provide a more authentic experience than a business that only publicly exhibits those values.[208]

Morgan continues that the technological environment accounts for roughly 30% of the employee's experience. Access to effective, up-to-date, and easily implementable technology will allow employees to grow

---

[208] Morgan, 2017

their skills and be highly engaged during their working hours. The final factor accounting for the final 40% of the employee experience is the cultural environment in which Morgan describes as follows for a company that exhibits a strong office culture:

1. The company is viewed positively by employees, clients, customers, and investors.
2. Everyone, employees, managers, and customers, all feel valued.
3. Employees feel a legitimate sense of purpose and feel as though they are part of a diverse and inclusive team.
4. Referrals come from inside the company and employees. If employees feel as though they can recommend their place of business, it will resonate with future employees and customers because they trust their organization enough to recommend it to their friends and acquaintances.
5. The company treats all employees fairly and provides them with the opportunity to learn new things and have readily available access to the resources to do so.
6. The organization is dedicated to the health and wellness of everyone, while executives and managers serve as coaches and mentors. [209]

With these three factors defined, here are the nine types of companies or organizations you will likely discover in your job search:

1. Inexperienced – these companies do not actively invest in any of the three factors: technological, physical, or cultural.
2. Technology Emergent – These businesses focus on offering the latest emerging technologies and fail to provide the other two factors.
3. Physically Emergent – Companies will provide beautiful workspaces but lack the technology and cultural aspects.
4. Culturally Emergent – These businesses will have a great feeling of energy and mood from their employees but may not offer much in terms of technology and physical environments.

---

[209] Morgan, 2017

5. Engaged – These companies focus on physical and cultural attributes.
6. Empowered – Great technology and cultural offerings are available to employees while the physical environment lacks quality.
7. Enabled – Physical and technological environments excel while the cultural experience lacks.
8. Pre-Experiential – Overall, the company is doing well but has not reached an exceptional level in all three areas.
9. Experiential – These companies or organizations exhibit exceptional expertise in all three areas of technology, physical, and cultural attributes. [210]

The three key attributes or factors all combine to create truly experiential companies and foster healthy, productive, and engaging employee experiences. The built physical environment, technological and employee development environments, and psychologically safe, culturally diverse, and inclusive environments that exhibit healthy and effective communication methods offer ideal working conditions for today's young professionals. Once the ideal company or business has been selected and thoroughly evaluated, you can begin your journey in defining yourself and your narrative – tailoring it to align with their mission and your personal values.

Following employment, you will find your own purpose and drive within your career. Morgan notes that for every year of experience, there is a correlating 0.6% decrease in happiness – but being equipped with employee development opportunities, investing in your future and retirement, and fostering healthy work environments can help eliminate this lack of happiness. Finding your own flow state at work will decrease the chance of becoming burnt out or emotionally and physically exhausted from unhealthy working conditions. [211]

Carefully consider the businesses in which you apply for interviews. Choose areas that show potential for growth and job stability should be evaluated in parallel with the health of the organization. Next, define

---

[210] Morgan, 2017
[211] Morgan, 2017

yourself through your resume and portfolio, and present yourself well during the interview with your REV points. Once hired, exhibit effective and civil communication styles, be proactive in your career path, and negotiate your employment terms. Plan for your future and retirement. As your progress through your own career phases, coach, and mentor the next generations to follow your own steps to develop their own career choices and decisions. With an emphasis on mindful, purposeful, and meaning-filled experiences, we can shape the future of work and generations to come – and helping the next generation of young professionals.

Sources

Sources & Continued Reading

Young Professionals are encouraged to read the following publications noted below:

16Personalities.com Sources:

"Architect Personality." 16Personalities, www.16personalities.com/intj-careers.

"Logician Personality." 16Personalities, www.16personalities.com/intj-careers.

"Commander Personality." 16Personalities, www.16personalities.com/entj-careers.

"Debater Personality." 16Personalities, www.16personalities.com/entp-careers.

"Advocate Personality." 16Personalities, www.16personalities.com/infj-careers.

"Mediator Personality." 16Personalities, www.16personalities.com/infp-careers.

"Protagonist Personality." 16Personalities, www.16personalities.com/enfj-careers.

"Campaigner Personality." 16Personalities, www.16personalities.com/enfp-careers.

"Logistician Personality." 16Personalities, www.16personalities.com/istj-careers.

"Defender Personality." 16Personalities, www.16personalities.com/isfj-careers.

"Executive Personality." 16Personalities, www.16personalities.com/estj-careers.

"Consul Personality." 16Personalities, www.16personalities.com/esfj-careers.

"Virtuoso Personality." 16Personalities, www.16personalities.com/istp-careers.

"Adventurer Personality." 16Personalities, www.16personalities.com/isfp-careers.

"Entrepreneur Personality." 16Personalities, www.16personalities.com/estp-careers.

"Entertainer Personality." 16Personalities, www.16personalities.com/esfp-careers.

Publication Sources:

Anderson, C. J. (2018). *TED talks: The official TED guide to public speaking.* Nicholas Brealey Publishing.

Berger, W. (2019). *A more beautiful question: The power of inquiry to spark breakthrough ideas.* Langara College.

Buckingham, M., & Goodall, A. (2019). *Nine lies about work: A free-thinking leader's guide to the real world.* Harvard Business Press.

Cain, S. (2013). *Quite: The power of introverts in a world that can't stop talking.* Penguin Books.

Caprino, K. (2020). *The most powerful you: 7 bravery-boosting paths to career bliss.* Murdoch Books.

Cenedella, M. (2019). *Ladder's 2019 resume guide .* Ladders, Inc.

Chapman, G. (2007). *The 5 languages of appreciation: Empowering organizations by encouraging people.* Moody Publishers.

Citrin, J. M. (2015). *The career playbook: Essential advice for today's aspring young professional.* Crown Business.

Clifton, J., & Harter, J. K. (2019). *It's the manager: Gallup finds the quality of managers and team leaders is the single biggest factor in your organization's long-term success.* Gallup Press.

Collins, J., & Porras, J. I. (2005). *Built to last: Successful habits of visionary companies.* Random House Business Books.

Coyle, D. (2019). *The culture code: The secrets of highly successful groups.* Bantam Books.

Coyle, D. (2012). *The little book of talent.* Random House Publishing Group.

Csikszentmihalyi, M. (2004). *Good business: Leadership, flow, and the making of meaning.* Penguin Publishing Group.

Durkeim, E. (2014). *The division of labor in society.* Free Press.

Ferrazzi, K., & Weyrich, N. (2020). *Leading without authority: How the new power of co-elevation can break down silos, transform teams, and reinvent collaboration.* Currency.

Gladwell, M. (2015). *The tipping point: How little things can make a big difference.* Abacus.

Grant, A. (2014). *Give and take: A revolutionary approach to success.* Weidenfeld & Nicolson.

Horowitz, B. (2014). *The hard thing about hard things: Building a business when there are no easy answers.* Harper Business.

Horowitz, B. (2019). *What you do is who you are: How to create your business culture.* Harper Business.

Johnson, S. K. (2020). *Inclusify: The power of uniqueness and belonging to build innovative teams.* Harper Business.

Kane, B. M. (2018). *One million followers: How I built a massive social following in 30 days: Growth hacks for your business, your message, and your brand from the world's greatest minds.* BenBella Books.

Kaye, B., & Winkle-Giulioni, J. (2019). *Help them grow or watch them go: Career conversations organizations need and employees want.* Berrett-Koehler Publishers, Inc.

Kelley, T. (2017). *Get that job!: The quick & complete guide to a winning job interview.* Plovercrest Press.

King, M. (2021). *Social chemistry: Decoding the patterns of human connection.* Dutton.

Lencioni, P. (2012). *The advantage: Why organizational health trumps everything else in business.* Wiley.

Levitt, S. D., & Dubner, S. J. (2014). *Freakonomics.* Denoel.

Livingston, J. (2016). *No more work: Why full time employment is a bad idea.* The University of North Carolina Press.

Lowry, E. (2019). *Broke millennial takes on investing: A beginner's guide to leveling up uour money.* Penguin Publishing Group.

McGovern, M. (2017). *Thriving in the gig economy: How to capitalize and compete in the new world of work.* Weiser.

Moon, Y. M. (2011). *Different: Escaping the competitive hard.* Crown.

Parker, P. (2020). *The art of gathering: Why we meet and why it matters.* Penguin Publishing Group.

Petersen, A. H. (2021). *CAN'T EVEN: How millennials became the burnout generation.* Mariner Books.

Piesman, M., & Hartley, M. (1985). *The yuppie handbook: The state-of-the-art manual for young urban professionals.* Pocket Books.

Pink, D. (2019). *When: The scientific secrets of perfect timing.* Riverhead Books.

Porath, C. L. (2016). *Mastering civility: A manifesto for the workplace.* Grand Central Publishing.

Rose, T., & Ogas, O. (2020). *Dark horse: Achieving success through the pursuit of happiness.* Harper One.

Smith, A. (2011). *The wealth of nations.* Tantor.

Suzman, J. (2021). *Work: A deep history from the Stone Age to the Age of Robots.* Penguin Press.

Taylor, P. (2016). *The next America: Boomers, millennials, and the looming generational showdown.* PublicAffairs.

Wright, C. (2020). *The hidden habits of genius: Beyond talent, IQ, and grit - Unlocking the secrets of greatness.* Dey Street Book.

Wikipedia Sources:

"Good to Great." Wikipedia, Wikimedia Foundation, 7 June 2021, en.wikipedia.org/wiki/Good_to_Great.

"Abbott Laboratories." Wikipedia, Wikimedia Foundation, 3 Sept. 2021, en.wikipedia.org/wiki/Abbott_Laboratories.

"Circuit City." Wikipedia, Wikimedia Foundation, 1 Aug. 2021, en.wikipedia.org/wiki/Circuit_City.

"Fannie Mae." Wikipedia, Wikimedia Foundation, 14 Aug. 2021, en.wikipedia.org/wiki/Fannie_Mae.

"Gillette." Wikipedia, Wikimedia Foundation, 2 Sept. 2021, en.wikipedia.org/wiki/Gillette.

"Kimberly-Clark." Wikipedia, Wikimedia Foundation, 26 Aug. 2021, en.wikipedia.org/wiki/Kimberly-Clark.

"Kroger." Wikipedia, Wikimedia Foundation, 3 Sept. 2021, en.wikipedia.org/wiki/Kroger.

"Nucor." Wikipedia, Wikimedia Foundation, 2 Sept. 2021, en.wikipedia.org/wiki/Nucor.

"Altria." Wikipedia, Wikimedia Foundation, 3 Sept. 2021, en.wikipedia.org/wiki/Altria.

"Pitney Bowes." Wikipedia, Wikimedia Foundation, 4 July 2021, en.wikipedia.org/wiki/Pitney_Bowes.

"Walgreens." Wikipedia, Wikimedia Foundation, 21 Aug. 2021, en.wikipedia.org/wiki/Walgreens.

"Wells Fargo." Wikipedia, Wikimedia Foundation, 4 Sept. 2021, en.wikipedia.org/wiki/Wells_Fargo.

Bibliography

1. Piesman, M., & Hartley, M. (1985). *The yuppie handbook: The state-of-the-art manual for young urban professionals.* Pocket Books.

2. Baby Boomers (born from 1946 to 1964). As exuberant youths led the countercultural upheavals of the 1960s. But the iconic image of that era – long-haired hippie protesters – describes only a portion of the cohort. Now on the front stoop of old age, Boomers are gloomy about their lives, worried about retirement, and wondering why they aren't young anymore. Icons: Bill and Hillary Clinton, George W. Bush, Barack Obama, Steve Jobs, Tom Hanks.

   > From *The Next America* by Paul Taylor, copyright © 2013. Reprinted by permission of Public Affairs, an imprint of Hatchette Book Group, Inc.

3. The Millennials (born after 1980). Empowered by digital technology; coddled by parents; respectful of elders; slow to adulthood; conflict-averse; at ease with racial, ethnic, and sexual diversity; confident in their economic futures despite coming of age in bad times. Icons: Mark Zuckerberg, Lena Dunham, LeBron James, Carrie Underwood, Jennifer Lawrence, Lady Gaga.

   > From *The Next America* by Paul Taylor, copyright © 2013. Reprinted by permission of Public Affairs, an imprint of Hatchette Book Group, Inc.

4. "Views of Business: Millennials' views of business are not substantially different from those of older generations. On a three-question index of attitudes about business power and profits, Millennials' opinions mirror those of Gen Xers and members of the Silent Generation and are slightly less critical of business than are the view of Baby Boomers. Also, Millennials are about as likely as other cohorts to agree that the country's strength is built mostly on the success of American business."

   > From *The Next America* by Paul Taylor, copyright © 2013. Reprinted by permission of Public Affairs, an imprint of Hatchette Book Group, Inc.

5. "OLD WORK RULE: Your team is limited to those who report to you or report to your manager. NEW WORK RULE: Your team is made up of everyone – inside and outside the company – important to achieving your project or mission."
   "OLD WORK RULE: Professional relationships happen organically over time and develop without purposeful effort. NEW WORK RULE: Professional relationships must be proactively and authentically developed with the people on your teams. This is the new competency of collaboration and productivity. It is critical to getting things done, more quickly."
   "OLD WORK RULE: Leadership is something bestowed upon by the company or organization. It comes with the authority associated with your job title. NEW WORK

RULE: Leadership is everyone's responsibility. You must help lead your team, regardless of your job title or level of authority."

"OLD WORK RULE: To advance in your career, you must do what's expected of you according to your job description. NEW WORK RULE: To advance in your career, you should do whatever it takes to create value for your team and your organization, even if it's not expected and even if it goes beyond your job description."

"OLD WORK RULE: To convince your teammates to tackle a project or mission, you must make a passionate and persuasive case for it. NEW WORK RULE: To invite your teammates to join your project or mission, you must first earn permission to lead through serving, sharing, and caring."

"OLD WORK RULE: When it came to growing professionally and developing both hard and soft skills, you looked to your manager, and to performance reviews and training programs. As a manager yourself, you generally only offered developmental feedback to someone who was formally assigned to you as a direct report. NEW WORK RULE: We seek out our team for development and growth. We offer teammates the candid feedback they need to develop and improve their skills, performance, and behavior because we are committed to their success and to the success of the greater mission."

6. "The epoch that you yourself were born into commenced in the early twentieth century, as Western society transitioned into a factory-based manufacturing economy. That epoch is often dubbed the Industrial Age, but it would be more apt to call it the Age of Standardization... We are experiencing this shift to the personal in our workplaces. Society is transitioning from an industrial economy dominated by large, stable, hierarchical organizations to an increasingly diverse and decentralized knowledge-and-service economy populated by freelancers, independent contractors, and free agents."

7. "In 2018, the nonprofit think tank Populace conducted a national survey through Luntz Global that questioned a demographically representative sample... When the participants were asked what constituted society's definition of success, the two most common responses by far were wealth and status. But when asked if they agreed with this definition, only 18 percent reported completely or mostly... about what kind of person was considered most successful: though 74 percent declared that according to society's definition it was "someone who is powerful," 91 percent said that for them personally, it was "someone who is purpose-driven."

Exerpt(s) from *Leading without authority: How the new power of co-elevation can break down silos, transform teams, and reinvent collaboration* by Keith Ferrazzi with Noel Weyrich, copyright © 2020 by Keith Ferrazzi. Used by permission of Currency, an imprint of Randome House, a division of Penguin Random House LLC. All rights reserved.

8. "The closest thing to a universal definition of "work" – one that... it involves purposefully expending energy or effort on a task to achieve a goal or end... At its most fundamental, work is always an energy transaction and the capacity to do certain kinds of work is what distinguishes living organisms from dead..."

Excerpt(s) from *Work: A Deep History, from the Stone Age to the Age of Robots* by James Suzman, copyright © 2020 by James Suzman. Used by permission of Penguin Press, an imprint of Penguin Publishing Group, a division of Penguin Random House LLC. All rights reserved.

9. *Work: A Deep History, from the Stone Age to the Age of Robots* by James Suzman

10. *Work: A Deep History, from the Stone Age to the Age of Robots* by James Suzman

11. "He asserted that legal regulations, that is, rules of conduct that are sanctioned, can be roughly divided into two major types: repressive sanctions, which are characteristic of penal law and involve punishment for transgressions and deviance; and restitutive sanctions, which, in contrast do not rely on punishment but rather rely on righting of a balance upset by the violation." p. xvii

Durkeim, Emile. 2014. *The Division of Labor in Society. New York : New York: Free Press, 2014.*

12. "The predominance of penal or restitutive law in given societies, Durkheim argued, could serve as an index of the type of society, or the type of solidarity under consideration. Societies based on mechanical solidarity relied almost exclusively on penal sanctions. What was punished was departure from the collective way of life, the shared values, and beliefs of the society. Any action that was perceived as an infringement of the collective consciousness – the shared mental and moral orientations of societies – was conceived as a crime and sanctioned accordingly. In modern societies, on the other hand, in which individuality, and hence the violation of individual rights, is central, restitutive rather than penal sanctions predominate." p. xvii

> Durkheim, Emile. 2014. The Division of Labor in Society. New York : New York: Free Press, 2014.

13. "... a fourth of the adults actually employed in the United States are paid wages lower than would lift them above the official poverty line—and so a fourth of American children live in poverty. Almost half of employed adults in this country are eligible for food stamps."

> Livingston, James. No More Work (p. 17). The University of North Carolina Press. Kindle Edition.

14. "... two-thirds of existing jobs, including those involving "non-routine cognitive tasks"... are at risk of death by computerization within twenty years."

> Livingston, James. *No More Work* (p. 17). The University of North Carolina Press. Kindle Edition.

15. The fastest-growing component of household income since 1959 has been "transfer payments" from government. By the turn of the twenty-first century, 20 percent of all household income came from this source... Without this income supplement, half of the adults with full-time jobs would live below the poverty line, and most working Americans would be eligible for food stamps."

> Livingston, James. *No More Work* (p. 17). The University of North Carolina Press. Kindle Edition.

16. "... the husbands cut their work week by slightly less than an hour... The wives cut five hours off their work week, but they spent that "free" time with their children... The women reduced their labor force participation rates as nominal family income rose, in other words, choosing more time over more income, in an exact inversion of what has happened in the workplace since the 1980s. When given a choice, the working mothers leaned in to spend time with their children."

> Livingston, James. *No More Work* (p. 17). The University of North Carolina Press. Kindle Edition.

"... it would be cheaper than welfare: "The Family Assistance Program, excluding the Day Care Program and Work Training Provisions, can be administered at an

annual cost per family of $72 to $96. Similar costs for the current welfare system run
between $200 and $300 annually per family."

Livingston, James. *No More Work* (pp. 17-18). The University of
North Carolina Press. Kindle Edition.

17. "According to a recent RAND-Princeton University study, from 2005 to 2015 the
traditional workforce, people working in full-time jobs, didn't grow at all. Meanwhile
the population of people working in "alternative work arrangements" increased by 67
percent. The report concludes, "A striking implication of these estimates is that all of
the net employment growth in the U.S. economy appears to have occurred in
alternative work arrangements. [...] Eighty percent of individuals who make the
transition from traditional to indie work and last for 12 months on their own report
they can't imagine ever returning to a traditional job. This includes "involuntary"
soloists who went out on their own because they lost a job."

McGovern, M. (2017). *Thriving in the gig economy: How to
capitalize and compete in the new world of work.* Weiser.

18. "In the annual study of independent work by MBO Partners, an employment
platform, 47 percent of the independent workers in this age group felt that their prior
employer did not understand their value, and this was a factor contributing to their
decision to become independent."

McGovern, M. (2017). *Thriving in the gig economy: How to
capitalize and compete in the new world of work.* Weiser.

19. "Good to Great." Wikipedia, Wikimedia Foundation, 7 June 2021,
en.wikipedia.org/wiki/Good_to_Great.

20. "Altria." Wikipedia, Wikimedia Foundation, 3 Sept. 2021,
en.wikipedia.org/wiki/Altria.

21. "Wells Fargo." Wikipedia, Wikimedia Foundation, 4 Sept. 2021,
en.wikipedia.org/wiki/Wells_Fargo.

22. "Fannie Mae." Wikipedia, Wikimedia Foundation, 14 Aug. 2021,
en.wikipedia.org/wiki/Fannie_Mae.

23. "Circuit City." Wikipedia, Wikimedia Foundation, 1 Aug. 2021,
en.wikipedia.org/wiki/Circuit_City.

24. "Nucor." Wikipedia, Wikimedia Foundation, 2 Sept. 2021,
en.wikipedia.org/wiki/Nucor.

25. "Kroger." Wikipedia, Wikimedia Foundation, 3 Sept. 2021,
en.wikipedia.org/wiki/Kroger.

26. "Gillette." Wikipedia, Wikimedia Foundation, 2 Sept. 2021, en.wikipedia.org/wiki/Gillette.

27. "Abbott Laboratories." Wikipedia, Wikimedia Foundation, 3 Sept. 2021, en.wikipedia.org/wiki/Abbott_Laboratories.

28. "... there are roughly 6 million firms in the U.S... 4 million have four or fewer employees..."

> Clifton, J., & Harter, J. K. *It's the manager: Gallup finds the quality of managers and team leaders is the single biggest factor in your organization's long-term success.* Gallup Press. 2019.

"... just 15% of employees worldwide are engaged at work."

> Clifton, J., & Harter, J. K. *It's the manager: Gallup finds the quality of managers and team leaders is the single biggest factor in your organization's long-term success.* Gallup Press. 2019.

29. "Millennials and Generation Z don't just work for a paycheck – they want a purpose... they are pursuing development... they want coaches... they want ongoing conversations..."

> Clifton, J., & Harter, J. K. *It's the manager: Gallup finds the quality of managers and team leaders is the single biggest factor in your organization's long-term success.* Gallup Press. 2019.

30. "A 2016 survey of HR professionals by my old employer Deloitte found that just 24 percent of large companies with fifty thousand or more employees are relying on functionally organized hierarchies to get work done."

> Exerpt(s) from *Leading without authority: How the new power of co-elevation can break down silos, transform teams, and reinvent collaboration* by Keith Ferrazzi with Noel Weyrich, copyright © 2020 by Keith Ferrazzi. Used by permission of Currency, an imprint of Randome House, a division of Penguin Random House LLC. All rights reserved.

31. "Organizations the report said, 'are shifting their structures from traditional functional models toward inter-connected flexible teams.' The report continued, 'the entire concept of leadership is being radically redefined. The whole notion of positional leadership that people become leaders by virtue of their power or position is being challenged. Leaders are instead being asked to inspire team loyalty through the expertise, vision, and judgement.'"

32. "1. I am enthusiastic about the mission of the company. 2. I clearly understand what is expected of me. 3. I am surrounded by people who share my values. 4. I can use my strengths every day at work. 5. My teammates have my back. 6. I know I will be recognized for excellent work. 7. I have great confidence in my company's future. 8. In my work, I am always challenged to grow."

33. "These deal with the elements of a person's experience created in their back-and-forth interactions with others on the team – the communal experience of work. [...] These deal instead with the individual experience of work. [...] These two categories of experiences – we experiences and me experiences – are the things we need at work in order to thrive."

34. "Recently the ADP Research Institute conducted a nineteen-country study on the nature of engagement at work – what drives it, and what it drives. [...] First, virtually all work is in fact teamwork. In companies with over 150 employees, 82 percent of people work on teams, and 72 percent work on more than one team. Even in small companies, of fewer than twenty people, this finding holds: 68 percent of those in small companies report working on a team, and 49% say they work on more than one team. This proved to be so in every single country in the study."

35. "Second, we know that if you do happen to work on a team you are twice as likely to score high on the eight engagement items, and that this trend linking engagement to teams extends to multiple teams – in fact, the most engaged group of workers across the working world are those who work on five distinct teams. Third... those team members who said they trusted their team leader were twelve times more likely to be fully engaged at work."

Buckingham, M., & Goodall, A. (2019). *Nine lies about work: A free-thinking leader's guide to the real world.* Harvard Business Pres. Printed with Permission.

36. "[...] But what about our first lie, that people care which company they work for? Well, we now know that these eight questions measure very precisely those aspects of our experience of work that matter the most [...] then when we ask these eight questions to every person in every team at a particular company, we should get, generally, the same responses. [...] But that's not the case – in fact, it's never the case."

Buckingham, M., & Goodall, A. (2019). *Nine lies about work: A free-thinking leader's guide to the real world.* Harvard Business Pres. Printed with Permission.

37. "So, though you are told that the best plan wins, the reality is quite different. Many plans, particularly those created in large organizations, are overly generalized, quickly obsolete, and frustrating to those asked to execute them. It's far better to coordinate your team's efforts in real time, relying heavily on the informed, detailed intelligence of each unique team member."

Buckingham, M., & Goodall, A. (2019). *Nine lies about work: A free-thinking leader's guide to the real world.* Harvard Business Pres. Printed with Permission.

38. "Despite this evidence, however, it remains true that goals, and cascaded goals in particular, have an intuitive appeal to many leaders who find themselves in search of ways to ensure efficient and aligned execution in their organizations. And, at the same time, it also remains true that for those of us in the trenches, our experience of goals feels nonintuitive, mechanical, fake, even demeaning."

Buckingham, M., & Goodall, A. (2019). *Nine lies about work: A free-thinking leader's guide to the real world.* Harvard Business Pres. Printed with Permission.

39. "Which makes it all the more surprising (or frustrating, or depressing) that companies are not, in fact, built to help us pinpoint and then contribute our unique strengths. In their systems and processes and technologies, in their rituals and language and philosophies, they evidence exactly the opposite design: to measure us against a standardized model, and then badger us to become as similar to this model as possible. They are built, that is, around the lie that the best people are well-rounded."

Buckingham, M., & Goodall, A. (2019). *Nine lies about work: A free-thinking leader's guide to the real world.* Harvard Business Pres. Printed with Permission.

40. "Instead, what the workers were responding to was attention. Each of these interventions demonstrated to the workers that management was interested in them and their experience, and they liked that. [...] The truth, then, is that people need attention – and when you give it to us in a safe and nonjudgmental environment, we will come and stay and play and work."

Buckingham, M., & Goodall, A. (2019). *Nine lies about work: A free-thinking leader's guide to the real world.* Harvard Business Pres. Printed with Permission.

41. "How stupid you are depends on which part of the country you're standing in."

"Smokey and the Bandit." Directed by Hal Needham. Screenplay by James Lee Barrett, Charles Shyer, Alan Mandel. Story by Hal Needham and Robert L. Levy. Produced by Mort Engelberg and Robert L. Levy. 1977.

42. "None of the mechanisms and meetings – not the models, not the consensus sessions, not the exhaustive competencies, not the carefully calibrated rating scales – none of them will ensure that the truth of you emerges in the room, because all of them are based on the belief that people can reliably rate other people. And they can't."

Buckingham, M., & Goodall, A. (2019). *Nine lies about work: A free-thinking leader's guide to the real world.* Harvard Business Pres. Printed with Permission.

43. "As with all the lies we've addressed in the book so far, the lie that people have potential is a product of organizations' desire for control, and their impatience with individual differences. [...] By keeping these two ideas... mass and velocity... and by using momentum to describe their combination, we suddenly enable you, the team leader, to do all manner of useful things to help..."

Buckingham, M., & Goodall, A. (2019). *Nine lies about work: A free-thinking leader's guide to the real world.* Harvard Business Pres. Printed with Permission.

44. "Yet still, the assumption that pervades our working world is that "work is bad" and "life is good," and therefore work-life balance matters most. [...] Good intentions aside, the problems with all this begin with the concept of balance…"

Buckingham, M., & Goodall, A. (2019). *Nine lies about work: A free-thinking leader's guide to the real world.* Harvard Business Pres. Printed with Permission.

45. "Now, some might choose other attributes for their lists, but those above are a reasonable summary of the theory-world view of leadership. And the reason that this isn't a chapter on leadership is not that the qualities listed aren't useful (they are) or that this topic has been done to death (it's close) but, rather, that when we look critically, we realize that we may well have misunderstood leadership altogether. Indeed, the final lie that we encounter at work is that leadership is a thing."

Buckingham, M., & Goodall, A. (2019). *Nine lies about work: A free-thinking leader's guide to the real world.* Harvard Business Pres. Printed with Permission.

46. "Aspiration. This phase, beginning in your college years and continuing through your first years in the workforce, marks your transition into adulthood. It draws on everything you've learned in college and internships and all of the challenges you will meet or will have faced in your first exposures to the work world. The Aspiration Phase is about discovery and introspection, the process of learning, and the development of knowledge."

Excerpt(s) from *The Career Playbook: Essential advice for today's aspring young professional* by James M. Citrin © 2015 by Esaress International S. A. R. L. Used by permission of Crown Business, an imprint of Random House, a division of Penguin Random House LLC. All rights reserved.

47. "Promise. The Promise Phase begins with your first or second job and lasts through your early promotions and job changes. Chronologically, this phase tends to run from one or two years after graduation over the next seven to ten years of your career. During this stage, your value will begin to be recognized by those who employ you through your compensation, promotions, and access to the best assignments and mentors… One goal in this phase is to show that the bet your superiors made on your potential was well placed."

Excerpt(s) from *The Career Playbook: Essential advice for today's aspring young professional* by James M. Citrin © 2015 by Esaress International S. A. R. L. Used by permission of Crown Business, an imprint of Random House, a division of Penguin Random House LLC. All rights reserved.

48. "The Momentum Phase is when the value of your experience will overtake your potential value as you increase your professional standing by capitalizing on your experience, stature, skills, and expertise."

Excerpt(s) from *The Career Playbook: Essential advice for today's aspring young professional* by James M. Citrin © 2015 by Esaress International S. A. R. L. Used by permission of Crown Business, an imprint of Random House, a division of Penguin Random House LLC. All rights reserved.

49. "Architect Personality." 16Personalities, www.16personalities.com/intj-careers.

50. "Logician Personality." 16Personalities, www.16personalities.com/intj-careers.

51. "Commander Personality." 16Personalities, www.16personalities.com/entj-careers.

52. "Debater Personality." 16Personalities, www.16personalities.com/entp-careers.

53. "Advocate Personality." 16Personalities, www.16personalities.com/infj-careers.

54. "Mediator Personality." 16Personalities, www.16personalities.com/infp-careers.

55. "Protagonist Personality." 16Personalities, www.16personalities.com/enfj-careers.

56. "Campaigner Personality." 16Personalities, www.16personalities.com/enfp-careers.

57. "Logistician Personality." 16Personalities, www.16personalities.com/istj-careers.

58. "Defender Personality." 16Personalities, www.16personalities.com/isfj-careers.

59. "Executive Personality." 16Personalities, www.16personalities.com/estj-careers.

60. "Consul Personality." 16Personalities, www.16personalities.com/esfj-careers.

61. "Virtuoso Personality." 16Personalities, www.16personalities.com/istp-careers.

62. "Adventurer Personality." 16Personalities, www.16personalities.com/isfp-careers.

63. "Entrepreneur Personality." 16Personalities, www.16personalities.com/estp-careers.

64. "Entertainer Personality." 16Personalities, www.16personalities.com/esfp-careers.

65. "They discovered the weekly profits of the stores managed by extroverts were 16 percent higher than the profits of those led by introverts – but only when the employees were passive types who tended to do their job without exercising initiative. Introverted leaders had the exact opposite results. When they worked with employees who actively tried to improve work procedures, their stores outperformed those led by extroverts by more than 14 percent. […] When the followers were not proactive, though-when they simply did as the leader instructed-the teams led by extroverts outperformed those led by the introverts by 22 percent… But with their natural ability to inspire, extroverted leaders are better at getting results from more passive workers."

66. "1. He was deeply involved in the strategy and implementation, down to having his own mother adopt children from a conquered tribe to symbolize the integration process. 2. He started with the job description he needed to fill, be it cavalry, doctors, scholars, or engineers, and then went after the talent to fill it […] 3. Not only did he make sure that conquered people were treated equally, but through adoption and intermarriage, he made them kin. […] As a result, they felt truly equal – and they became more loyal to him […]"

67. "1. What is the gender of your target audience? […] 2. What is the age of your target audience? […] 3. What is your desired marketing goal? […] 4. Where is your audience located? […] 5. What interests do people who buy your product or brand have? […] 6. What is some additional lifestyle information you know about your audience? […] 7. Who are your top-level competitors and what do their fans look like in regard to the questions on this list?"

68. Anderson, C. *TED talks: The official TED guide to public* speaking.. Mariner Books, Houghton Mifflin Harcourt. *2016.*

69. Anderson, C. *TED talks: The official TED guide to public* speaking.. Mariner Books, Houghton Mifflin Harcourt. *2016.*

70. Anderson, C. *TED talks: The official TED guide to public* speaking.. Mariner Books, Houghton Mifflin Harcourt. *2016.*

71. Anderson, C. *TED talks: The official TED guide to public* speaking.. Mariner Books, Houghton Mifflin Harcourt. *2016.*

72. Anderson, C. *TED talks: The official TED guide to public* speaking.. Mariner Books, Houghton Mifflin Harcourt. *2016.*

73. Anderson, C. *TED talks: The official TED guide to public* speaking.. Mariner Books, Houghton Mifflin Harcourt. *2016.*

74. "1. What have been your ten greatest accomplishments? 2. What about your personal history has given you a unique perspective? 3. Think about yourself at a younger age – what did you enjoy doing? 4. What comes easily or naturally to you? 5. Consider praise from teachers, friends, colleagues – what was the praise referring to? 6. What negative or positive life events have shaped your life? 7. What are your values? 8. What are the areas you have received special training or experience? What about special praise? 9. What do you enjoy or love being? 10. Where have you made the biggest difference in someone's life?"

> Taken from *The most powerful you: 7 bravery-boosting paths to career bliss* by Kathy Caprino. Copyright 2020, by Kathy Caprino. Used by permission of Harper Collins Leadership. www.harpercollinsleadership.com

75. "1. People tend to believe that tasks or responsibilities that come easily to them seem unremarkable. 2. The jobs that people have gone badly have left them with a skewed perception. 3. People have not found a job or employment they are passionate about or enjoy and think they are to blame. 4. Employees are encouraged to believe they somehow were not remarkable."

> Taken from *The most powerful you: 7 bravery-boosting paths to career bliss* by Kathy Caprino. Copyright 2020, by Kathy Caprino. Used by permission of Harper Collins Leadership. www.harpercollinsleadership.com

76. Taken from *The most powerful you: 7 bravery-boosting paths to career bliss* by Kathy Caprino. Copyright 2020, by Kathy Caprino. Used by permission of Harper Collins Leadership. www.harpercollinsleadership.com

77. Cenedella, M. (2019). *Ladder's 2019 resume guide* . Ladders, Inc.

78. Cenedella, M. (2019). *Ladder's 2019 resume guide* . Ladders, Inc.

79. Cenedella, M. (2019). *Ladder's 2019 resume guide* . Ladders, Inc.
80. Cenedella, M. (2019). *Ladder's 2019 resume guide* . Ladders, Inc.

81. Cenedella, M. (2019). *Ladder's 2019 resume guide* . Ladders, Inc.

82. Cenedella, M. (2019). *Ladder's 2019 resume guide* . Ladders, Inc.

83. Cenedella, M. (2019). *Ladder's 2019 resume guide* . Ladders, Inc.

84. Cenedella, M. (2019). *Ladder's 2019 resume guide* . Ladders, Inc.

85. Cenedella, M. (2019). *Ladder's 2019 resume guide* . Ladders, Inc.

86. Cenedella, M. (2019). *Ladder's 2019 resume guide* . Ladders, Inc.

87. Cenedella, M. (2019). *Ladder's 2019 resume guide* . Ladders, Inc.

88. Cenedella, M. (2019). *Ladder's 2019 resume guide* . Ladders, Inc.

89. Cenedella, M. (2019). *Ladder's 2019 resume guide* . Ladders, Inc.

90. Cenedella, M. (2019). *Ladder's 2019 resume guide* . Ladders, Inc.

91. Cenedella, M. (2019). *Ladder's 2019 resume guide* . Ladders, Inc.

92. "Where a connoisseur can navigate a category with effortless intuition, a novice will struggle to find beginning, middle, or end."

> Excerpt(s) from *Different: Escaping the Competitive Herd* by Youngme Moon, copyright © 2010 by Youngme Moon. Used by permission of Crown Business, an imprint of Random House, a division of Penguin Random House LLC. All rights reserved.

"Connoisseurs have tremendous affection for the category and are discriminating with respect to their choices, but this doesn't necessarily lead to a particular brand preference. They are selective, informed, and picky, but they are variety seekers and bran samplers, too. Their loyalty is directed toward the category as opposed to any particular brand within it."

93. "Opportunists are akin to connoisseurs in one respect: they are brand-agnostic category experts. The difference is that when they participate in the category, they do so without joy. Opportunists are transaction-oriented consumers whose posture toward the category could almost be described as competitive."

94. "Pragmatics are non-differentiators; they no longer expend the energy to keep abreast of the latest competitive permutations in the market... an extreme version of a pragmatic would be an indifferent, someone who treats the category as almost pure commodity."

95.

96. "The final segment would consist of the brand loyalists. These are the folks, who despite the number of competitive alternatives in the market, still exhibit a stubborn passion for a particular brand."

97.

98.

100. "The first is what I like to call augmentation-by-addition. To the extent that a product (or a "value proposition") can be thought of as a set of benefits, product marketers will habitually look to improve it by bolstering those benefits. Sometimes, they'll do this by strengthening an already-existing benefit..."

101. "The second form of product augmentation is what I like to call augmentation-by-multiplication. Because companies recognize that different people have different preferences, they'll frequently hatch specialized versions of their product in an attempt to meet the needs of specific consumer segments."

102. "According to Liljenquist, advice seeking has four benefits: learning, perspective taking, commitment, and flattery."

103. "According to the U.S. Bureau of Labor Statistics, 70 percent of all jobs are found through networking… One hundred percent of the business leaders and 97 percent of the young professionals ranked relationships above their health, their personal impact, and their compensation in importance."

104. "The lowest common denominator of social connection is a dyad – the one-on-one relationships we form with a single individual."

105. "Expansionists have extraordinarily large networks, are well-known, and have an uncanny ability to work a room. However, they often have trouble maintaining social ties and leveraging them to create value for themselves or others. Brokers generate value by bringing together typically disconnected parties from different social worlds. Their networks have huge information benefits and are highly innovative, since the majority of new ideas come from recombination. Conveners build dense networks in which their friends are also friends. This type of network has outsize trust and reputational benefits."

106. "The same applies to social intelligence. Broadly defined, social intelligence is a set of interpersonal competencies that influence your ability to get along with others and successfully navigate social interactions. As Daniel Goleman, the author of a book by that name, wrote:" The ingredients of social intelligence I propose here can be organized into two broad categories: social awareness, what we sense about others – and social facility, what we then do with that awareness."

107. '1. Reconnect with old friends and reawaken dormant relationships... 2. Focus on your "super-connectors." These are the small number of friends and mentors through whom a disproportionate number of other friends and opportunities have come your way... 3. Seek to help others... Building Your Career When You're Not Building Your Career."

191

108. "The next time you walk in that room, instead of seeing a wall of people, look for small clusters, islands of people. They always exist and are often near a piece of furniture. Now look for an island with an odd number – one, three, five. You've just found your conversational partner. Your addition will create numerical balance."

109. "The Stickiness Factor says that there are specific ways of making a contagious message memorable; there are relatively simple changes in the presentation and structuring of information that can make a big difference in how much of an impact it makes."

110. "What makes someone a Connector? The first – and most obvious – criterion is that Connectors know lots of people. They are the kinds of people who know everyone."

111. "When we don't examine the deeper assumptions behind why we gather, we end up skipping too quickly to replicating old, staid formats of gathering. And we forgo the possibility of creating something memorable, even transformative... When people come together without any thought to their purpose, they create gatherings about nothing... they fail at the test for a meaningful reason for coming together..."

112. "The purpose-driven list. The guest list is the first test of a robust gathering purpose. It is the first chance to put your ideals into practice... Inviting people is easy.

Excluding people can be hard... You will have begun to gather with purpose when you learn to exclude with purpose..."

"Groups of 6: Groups of this rough size are wonderfully conductive to intimacy, high levels of sharing, and discussion through storytelling... Groups of 12 to 15: Twelve is small enough to build trust and intimacy, and small enough for a single moderator, if there is one, formal or informal, to handle... Groups of 30: Thirty starts to feel like a party, whether or not your gathering is one... Groups of 150: intimacy and trust is still palpable at the level of the whole group, and before it becomes an audience... Above the "tribe" number, it's still possible to gather well, of course, but the unit of experience usually gets broken up into smaller subgroups."

113. "The choice of place is often made according to every consideration but purpose... when you choose a venue for logistical reasons, you are letting those logistics override your purpose, when in fact they should be working for it... Priming. Before your event starts, it has begun. Your gathering begins at the moment your guests first learn of it."

114. "A recent poll showed that 50% of employers believe they know within the first five minutes of an interview whether a candidate is a good fit."

"I call these your "REV Points," because they work best if they're Relevant, Exceptional and Verifiable (REV). I'll say more about that later in the chapter."

115. "Relevant: A relevant qualification is in demand by employers. Study several job postings for the type of job you want, and underline the important skills, qualifications, and qualities the employer is looking for. Which seem to be the top priorities?"

> Kelley, Thea. *Get that job!: The quick and complete guide to a winning interview.* Plovercrest Press, 2017. Reprinted under Fair Use, Section 107 of the Copyright Act. Quote is shown to convey the original author's context.

"Exceptional: An exceptional quality or qualification is one that stands out. Probably all of your competitors have experience in multi-tasking. But can they all speak Mandarin with the company's Chinese clients?"

> Kelley, Thea. *Get that job!: The quick and complete guide to a winning interview.* Plovercrest Press, 2017. Reprinted under Fair Use, Section 107 of the Copyright Act. Quote is shown to convey the original author's context.

"Verifiable: By this I mean that the item is not just a claim or opinion. It's something you can prove or give evidence for."

> Kelley, Thea. *Get that job!: The quick and complete guide to a winning interview.* Plovercrest Press, 2017. Reprinted under Fair Use, Section 107 of the Copyright Act. Quote is shown to convey the original author's context.

116. "You may have seen acronyms like CAR (Challenge, Action, Results), PAR (Problem, Actions, Results) and SOAR (Situation, Obstacles, Actions, Results). Each of these acronyms provides a framework or model for telling a story. They're all good. ("Challenge," "Problem" and "Situation" all mean pretty much the same thing.)"

> Kelley, Thea. *Get that job!: The quick and complete guide to a winning interview.* Plovercrest Press, 2017. Reprinted under Fair Use, Section 107 of the Copyright Act. Quote is shown to convey the original author's context.

117. "Get your answer off to a good start. Often the best way to start is by combining one of your top REV points with a one- to three-sentence summary of your career. Mention the number of years of experience you have only if that number matches or moderately exceeds what the employer is looking for [...] Move on to another REV Point. [...] Continue until you have included all of your REV Points. Include an example or two to illustrate your claims. Put the "V" in Verifiable! But you don't need to prove every claim in this answer; it's more like a spot check. [...] Reveal yourself, without "TMI" (Too Much Information)! [...] Humor is a plus, as long as

it's absolutely inoffensive. [...] Plan a good ending. Otherwise, you may find yourself trailing off with something like "So yeah, that's about it." [...] Type it up in a neat, outline form. Use bullets and sub-bullets to help organize your thinking. Use abbreviations and symbols to make it concise and visual. The more you make it easy to read, the less it will intrude on the process of expressing yourself in a natural way. [...] Speak your REV Intro out loud, using the outline as your road map, and time yourself. Your intro should be no longer than one to two minutes. If it's longer, prune it down. Remember, this is just the start of the interview. [...] Adjust the outline as many times as you need to. [...] Now, practice without looking at the outline. (It may be helpful to memorize the outline. That's another reason for making the outline very concise and clear: it will be easier to memorize.) [...] Get feedback. [...] Practice with a buddy or a coach and ask for feedback on what worked well and what could be better."

Kelley, Thea. *Get that job!: The quick and complete guide to a winning interview.* Plovercrest Press, 2017. Reprinted under Fair Use, Section 107 of the Copyright Act. Quote is shown to convey the original author's context.

118. "The three Cs are Competence, Compatibility with the company culture, and Chemistry. Competence: Of course, the interviewer wants to make sure you can do the job and do it well. This is what we all tend to think the whole interview is about: whether the candidate has the necessary experience, technical skills, and soft skills. But actually, there's more. Compatibility with the company culture: They also want to make sure you'll work well in this particular environment, especially if it's quite different from the organizations you've worked in before. For example, some organizations are very hard-driving and competitive, while others are more collaborative; some are very hierarchical and formal, while others are more open and want everyone to be a leader. Show the employer that you understand and appreciate their company culture and will work well within it. If you have more experience with that type of culture than your resume indicates, clarify that. Chemistry: Last but not least, they want a sense that you'll "click" with the boss and team members and that they'll enjoy spending a big chunk of their waking hours with you, day after day. Don't underestimate or forget the importance of liking and being liked by the people you're meeting – all of them, including the receptionist, shuttle driver and so on. Much of this comes down to everyday things like friendly chitchat, showing an interest in people, active listening, and body language such as a firm handshake, eye contact and a warm smile. In many cases, chemistry is even more important than competence."

Kelley, Thea. *Get that job!: The quick and complete guide to a winning interview.* Plovercrest Press, 2017. Reprinted under Fair Use, Section 107 of the Copyright Act. Quote is shown to convey the original author's context.

119. "Failing to make eye contact. A full 67% of these managers reported they would be less likely to hire someone who doesn't look them in the eye. Too little eye contact can make a candidate seem insincere or insecure. Too much can feel domineering. If you make eye contact about 30-60% of the time – less when talking, more when listening – you should make a good impression. Failing to smile. Two points in the interview definitely call for a smile, to show friendliness and enthusiasm: at the beginning and the end. In between, smile when it feels natural to you, and when the interviewer smiles. (Did you know you can smile too much in an interview? A recent study by Northeastern University showed that too much smiling can give the impression you're not taking the interview seriously. In my experience, however, most people are more likely to not smile enough.) Playing with something on the table. This is distracting, drawing attention to your nervousness. Fidgeting in your seat. This, too, draws attention to nervousness. Bad posture. Slouching can communicate a lack of motivation, interest, and respect. Crossing your arms over your chest. This communicates defensiveness. Playing with your hair or touching your face. If you tend to play with your long hair, tie it back. And did you know that touching the mouth or nose is sometimes associated with lying? Weak handshake. A full, firm handshake feels welcoming and confident. Too many hand gestures. This was mentioned by only 11% of those surveyed. Please don't take this to mean you must never talk with your hands in interviews. A good rule of thumb is to do it about as much as the interviewer does. Too-strong handshake. Don't ignore this because it's at the bottom of the list. This writer has often felt a bit intimidated – or physically uncomfortable – with powerful handshakes. Be sensitive to the gender and size of the person you're shaking hands with!

> Kelley, Thea. *Get that job!: The quick and complete guide to a winning interview.* Plovercrest Press, 2017. Reprinted under Fair Use, Section 107 of the Copyright Act. Quote is shown to convey the original author's context.

"Putting together the appreciation, REV Points and enthusiastically asking for the job, the complete closing statement presented above takes about 60 seconds. It is important to keep this statement brief and not hold the interviewer hostage with a lengthy speech at this point."

> Kelley, Thea. *Get that job!: The quick and complete guide to a winning interview.* Plovercrest Press, 2017. Reprinted under Fair Use, Section 107 of the Copyright Act. Quote is shown to convey the original author's context.

120. "The best item to measure this anywhere in the world is: "There is someone at work who encourages my development…When 60% of your employees give a strong "yes" to this item, you have transformed your workplace and changed the world a little to a lot. "
(Clifton & Harter, 2019)

121. Kaye, B., & Winkle-Giulioni, J. (2019). *Help them grow or watch them go: Career conversations organizations need and employees want.* Berrett-Koehler Publishers, Inc.

122. "Gallup discovered that the No. 1 reason people change jobs today is "career growth opportunities."

> Clifton, J., & Harter, J. K. *It's the manager: Gallup finds the quality of managers and team leaders is the single biggest factor in your organization's long-term success.* Gallup Press. 2019.

123. "Three elements of career growth: 1. Opportunity to make a difference 2. Success 3. Fit with my career aspirations."

> Clifton, J., & Harter, J. K. *It's the manager: Gallup finds the quality of managers and team leaders is the single biggest factor in your organization's long-term success.* Gallup Press. 2019.

124. "Here are eight questions to get you started:
What are your recent successes?
What are you most proud of?
What rewards and recognition matter most to you?
How does your role make a difference?
How would you like to make a bigger difference?
How are you using your strengths in your current role?
How would you like to use your strengths in the future?
What knowledge and skills do you need to get to the next stage of your career?"

> Clifton, J., & Harter, J. K. *It's the manager: Gallup finds the quality of managers and team leaders is the single biggest factor in your organization's long-term success.* Gallup Press. 2019.

125. "In actuality, psychologists Michael Ross and Fiore Sicoly found that three out of every four couples add up to significantly more than 100 percent. Partners overestimate their own contributions. This is known as the responsibility bias: exaggerating our own contributions relative to others' inputs. It's a mistake to which takers are especially vulnerable, and it's partially driven by the desire to see and present ourselves positively. [...] But there's another factor at play that's both more powerful and more flattering: information discrepancy. We have more access to information about our own contributions than the contributions of others. We see all of our own efforts, but we only witness a subset of our partners' efforts. When we think about who deserves the credit, we have more knowledge of our own onctributions."

Excerpt(s) from *Give and Take: A revolutionary approach to success* by Adam Grant © 2013 by Adam Grant. Used by permission of Viking Books, an imprint of Penguin Publishing Group, a division of Penguin Random House LLC. All Rights Reserved.

126. "As previously noted, each of us has a primary and secondary language of appreciation. Our primary language communicates more deeply to us than the others. Although we will accept appreciation in all five languages, we will not feel truly encouraged unless the message is communicated through our primary language. When messages are sent repeatedly in ways outside of that language, the intent of the message misses the mark and loses the impact the sender had hoped for."

Chapman, G. (2007). *The 5 languages of appreciation: Empowering organizations by encouraging people.* Moody Publishers printed with permission.

127. Chapman, G. (2007). *The 5 languages of appreciation: Empowering organizations by encouraging people.* Moody Publishers printed with permission.

128. Chapman, G. (2007). *The 5 languages of appreciation: Empowering organizations by encouraging people.* Moody Publishers.

129. Chapman, G. (2007). *The 5 languages of appreciation: Empowering organizations by encouraging people.* Moody Publishers.

130. "Hindsight conversations help others look backward and inward to determine who they are, where they've been, what they love, and where they excel."

Kaye, B., & Winkle-Giulioni, J. (2019). *Help them grow or watch them go: Career conversations organizations need and employees want.* Berrett-Koehler Publishers, Inc.

131. "Foresight conversations are designed to keep employees looking forward and outward toward changes, trends, and the ever-evolving big picture."

Kaye, B., & Winkle-Giulioni, J. (2019). *Help them grow or watch them go: Career conversations organizations need and employees want.* Berrett-Koehler Publishers, Inc.

132. "Leveraging the insights that surface from the convergence of hindsight and foresight [...] How do the employee's strengths fit into where the organization or industry is going?"

Kaye, B., & Winkle-Giulioni, J. (2019). *Help them grow or watch them go: Career conversations organizations need and employees want.* Berrett-Koehler Publishers, Inc.

133. "1. Start by explaining that a solid career future is based upon an understanding of who you are and what got you to where you are. 2. With the employee, create a list of the various positions, roles, and jobs they have held. 3. For each position, role, or job, ask the following questions: which parts brought you joy, energy, and a sense of persistence? Which parts led to boredom, disengagement, and a sense of just going through the motions? 4. Step back with the employee and see what themes emerge."

Kaye, B., & Winkle-Giulioni, J. (2019). *Help them grow or watch them go: Career conversations organizations need and employees want.* Berrett-Koehler Publishers, Inc.

"The five conversations that drive performance: 1 role and relationship orientation... 2. quick connect... 3. check-in... 4. developmental coaching... 5. progress reviews."

Kaye, B., & Winkle-Giulioni, J. (2019). *Help them grow or watch them go: Career conversations organizations need and employees want.* Berrett-Koehler Publishers, Inc.

134. "And the best plans are really collaborative development deals you strike with the employee. Make sure your DEAL is documented, employee owned, aligned with their goals, and linked to the needs of your organization."

Kaye, B., & Winkle-Giulioni, J. (2019). *Help them grow or watch them go: Career conversations organizations need and employees want.* Berrett-Koehler Publishers, Inc.

135. "But they do practice their own brand of ESP: Ever Scanning and Pondering. [...] ESP is a set of habits – habits that you can help employees build through ongoing foresight conversations.

Kaye, B., & Winkle-Giulioni, J. (2019). *Help them grow or watch them go: Career conversations organizations need and employees want.* Berrett-Koehler Publishers, Inc.

136. "It can be a hard sell – but recalibration is frequently the best way for employees to progress forward toward their goals. There's also the option of growing in place […] Clearly, up is not the only way. And even if up is the preferred destination, the climbing wall – the business environment in which we all operate – offers lots of ways to get there."

Kaye, B., & Winkle-Giulioni, J. (2019). *Help them grow or watch them go: Career conversations organizations need and employees want.* Berrett-Koehler Publishers, Inc.

137. "Education – the nearly unlimited sources of information and learning that can be formally or informally accessed. Exposure – the opportunities to learn from and through others via observation, mentorship, and more. Experience – action-based opportunities to learn by doing."

Kaye, B., & Winkle-Giulioni, J. (2019). *Help them grow or watch them go: Career conversations organizations need and employees want.* Berrett-Koehler Publishers, Inc.

138. "TIP #1: STARE AT WHO YOU WANT TO BECOME […] Studies show that even a brief connection with a role model can vastly increase unconscious motivation. For example, being told that you share a birthday with a mathematician can improve the amount of effort you're willing to put into difficult math tasks by 62 percent."

Excerpt(s) from *The Little Book of Talent: 52 tips for improving your skills* by Daniel Coyle © 2012 by Daniel Coyle. Used by Permission of Bantam Books, an imprint of Random House, a division of Penguin Random House LLC. All rights reserved.

139. "TIP #2: SPEND FIFTEEN MINUTES A DAY ENGRAVING THE SKILL ON YOUR BRAIN […] What's the best way to begin to learn a new skill? Is it by listening to a teacher's explanation? Reading an instructional book? Just leaping in and trying it out? […] Basically, they watch the skill being performed, closely and with great intensity, over and over, until they build a high-definition mental blueprint.

Excerpt(s) from *The Little Book of Talent: 52 tips for improving your skills* by Daniel Coyle © 2012 by Daniel Coyle. Used by Permission of Bantam Books, an imprint of Random House, a division of Penguin Random House LLC. All rights reserved.

140. "TIP #3: STEAL WITHOUT APOLOGY […] We are often told that talented people acquire their skill by following their "natural instincts." This sounds nice, but in fact it is baloney. All improvement is about absorbing and applying new information, and the best source of information is top performers. So, steal it."

Excerpt(s) from *The Little Book of Talent: 52 tips for improving your skills* by Daniel Coyle © 2012 by Daniel Coyle. Used by Permission of Bantam Books, an imprint of Random House, a division of Penguin Random House LLC. All rights reserved.

141. "TIP #4: BUY A NOTEBOOK [...] A high percentage of top performers keeps some form of daily performance journal."

142. "TIP #5: BE WILLING TO BE STUPID."

143. "TIP #6: CHOOSE SPARTAN OVER LUXURIOUS [...] We love comfort. We love state-of-the-art practice facilities, oak-paneled corner offices, spotless locker rooms, and fluffy towels. Which is a shame, because luxury is a motivational narcotic: It signals our unconscious minds to give less effort. It whispers, Relax, you've made it."

144. "TIP #7: BEFORE YOU START, FIGURE OUT IF IT'S A HARD SKILL OR A SOFT SKILL [...] The first step toward building a skill is to figure out exactly what type of skill you're building. Every skill falls into one of two categories: hard skills and soft skills. HARD, HIGH-PRECISION SKILLS are actions that are performed as correctly and consistently as possible, every time. They are skills that have one path to an ideal result; skills that you could imagine being performed by a reliable robot. Hard skills are about repeatable precision, and tend to be found in specialized pursuits, particularly physical ones. [...] SOFT, HIGH-FLEXIBILITY SKILLS, on the other hand, are those that have many paths to a good result, not just one. These skills aren't about doing the same thing perfectly every time, but rather about being agile and interactive; about instantly recognizing patterns as they unfold and making smart, timely choices."

145. "TIP #12: FIVE WAYS TO PICK A HIGH-QUALITY TEACHER OR COACH [...]
Great teachers, coaches, and mentors, like any rare species, can be identified by a few
characteristic traits. The following rules are designed to help you sort through the
candidates and make the best choice for yourself. 1) Avoid Someone Who Reminds
You of a Courteous Waiter. 2) Seek Someone Who Scares You a Little. 3) Seek
Someone Who Gives Short, Clear Directions. 4) Seek Someone Who Loves Teaching
Fundamentals. 5) Other Things Being Equal, Pick the Older Person."

146. "TIP #15: BREAK EVERY MOVE DOWN INTO CHUNKS [...] From the time
we're small, we hear this good advice from our parents and teachers: Take it a little
bit at a time. This advice works because it accurately reflects the way our brains learn.
Every skill is built out of smaller pieces—what scientists call chunks."

147. "TIP #17: EMBRACE STRUGGLE [...] I saw the same facial expression: eyes
narrow, jaw tight, nostrils flared, the face of someone intently reaching for something,
falling short, and reaching again. This is not a coincidence. Deep practice has a telltale
emotional flavor, a feeling that can be summed up in one word: "struggle.""

148. "TIP #20: PRACTICE ALONE [...] Solo practice works because it's the best way to
1) seek out the sweet spot at the edge of your ability, and 2) develop discipline,
because it doesn't depend on others."

149. "TIP #38: STOP BEFORE YOU'RE EXHAUSTED [...] In many skills, particularly athletic, medical, and military ones, there's a long tradition of working until total exhaustion. This tradition has its uses, particularly for improving fitness and mental toughness, and for forging emotional connections within a group. But when it comes to learning, the science is clear: Exhaustion is the enemy. Fatigue slows brains. It triggers errors, lessens concentration, and leads to shortcuts that create bad habits. It's no coincidence that most talent hotbeds put a premium on practicing when people are fresh, usually in the morning, if possible. When exhaustion creeps in, it's time to quit."

Excerpt(s) from *The Little Book of Talent: 52 tips for improving your skills* by Daniel Coyle © 2012 by Daniel Coyle. Used by Permission of Bantam Books, an imprint of Random House, a division of Penguin Random House LLC. All rights reserved.

150. "TIP #41 [...] END ON A POSITIVE NOTE A practice session should end like a good meal—with a small, sweet reward."

Excerpt(s) from *The Little Book of Talent: 52 tips for improving your skills* by Daniel Coyle © 2012 by Daniel Coyle. Used by Permission of Bantam Books, an imprint of Random House, a division of Penguin Random House LLC. All rights reserved.

151. (Smith, 2011)

152. (Smith, 2011)

153. (Smith, 2011)

154. "...when there are a lot of people willing and able to do a job, that job generally doesn't pay well. This is one of four meaningful factors that determine a wage. The others are the specialized skills a job requires, the unpleasantness of a job, and the demand for services that the job fulfills."
Levitt, S. D., & Dubner, S. J. 2014. *Freakonomics.* Denoel.

155. Wright, C. (2020). *The hidden habits of genius: Beyond talent, IQ, and grit - Unlocking the secrets of greatness.* Dey Street Books.

156. "Wright, C. (2020). *The hidden habits of genius: Beyond talent, IQ, and grit - Unlocking the secrets of greatness.* Dey Street Books.

157. Wright, C. (2020). *The hidden habits of genius: Beyond talent, IQ, and grit - Unlocking the secrets of greatness.* Dey Street Books.

158. "In a PayScale salary survey, 57 percent of respondents said that they'd never negotiated a salary in their current field, and the key reasons given amounted to fear: fear of losing their jobs, looking pushy, and feeling uncomfortable doing it."

> Taken from *The most powerful you: 7 bravery-boosting paths to career bliss* by Kathy Caprino. Copyright 2020, by Kathy Caprino. Used by permission of Harper Collins Leadership. www.harpercollinsleadership.com

159. "Many studies have confirmed this. New York Times bestselling authors Joseph Grenny and David Maxfield validated that gender bias in the workplace is real, finding that women' perceived competency drops by 35 percent and their perceived worth falls by $15,088 when they are judged as being "forceful" or "assertive." Compare this with the drops in competency and worth that men experience when being judged as forceful: their competency drops by 22 percent and their worth falls by $6,547."

> Taken from *The most powerful you: 7 bravery-boosting paths to career bliss* by Kathy Caprino. Copyright 2020, by Kathy Caprino. Used by permission of Harper Collins Leadership. www.harpercollinsleadership.com

160. "Uniqueness + belonging = inclusion."

> ... from *Inclusify: The power of uniqueness and belonging to build innovative teams* by Stefanie K. Johnson. Copyright © 2020 by Stefanie K. Johnson. Used by permission of HarperCollins Publishers.

161. "To start you on the path to overcoming your biases, I have created the ABCs of Breaking Bias: Admit it, Block it, Count it."

> ... from *Inclusify: The power of uniqueness and belonging to build innovative teams* by Stefanie K. Johnson. Copyright © 2020 by Stefanie K. Johnson. Used by permission of HarperCollins Publishers.

162. "For example, a group of venture capitalists is 25 percent less likely to invest successfully when all members are of the same race than when there is diversity on the team... Research from Deloitte shows that more inclusive organizations are six times as likely to be innovative, six times as likely to anticipate change and respond effectively, and twice as likely to meet or exceed financial targets."

> ... from *Inclusify: The power of uniqueness and belonging to build innovative teams* by Stefanie K. Johnson. Copyright © 2020 by Stefanie K. Johnson. Used by permission of HarperCollins Publishers.

163. "For every dollar of wealth held by white people in the United States, black families have 5 cents. Hispanic people have 6 cents."

> ... from *Inclusify: The power of uniqueness and belonging to build innovative teams* by Stefanie K. Johnson. Copyright © 2020 by Stefanie K. Johnson. Used by permission of HarperCollins Publishers.

164. "As of 2019, women and POC comprise only 25 percent and 27 percent of executives, respectively. Only 5 percent of CEOs are women. Five percent! This is despite the fact that women make up 51 percent of the population and minorities make up 39 percent of the population."

> ... from *Inclusify: The power of uniqueness and belonging to build innovative teams* by Stefanie K. Johnson. Copyright © 2020 by Stefanie K. Johnson. Used by permission of HarperCollins Publishers.

165. "Visionary companies develop, promote, and carefully select managerial talent grown from inside the company to a greater degree than the comparison companies. They do this as a key step in preserving their core. Over the period 1806 to 1992, we found evidence that only two visionary companies (11.1 percent) ever hired a chief executive directly from outside the company, compared to thirteen (72.2 percent) of the comparison companies. Of 113 chief executives for which we have data in the visionary companies, only 3.5 percent came directly from outside the company, versus 22.1 percent of 140 CEOs at the comparison companies. In other words, the visionary companies were six times more likely to promote insiders to chief executive than the comparison companies."

Collins, J., & Porras, J. I. (2005). *Built to last: Successful habits of visionary companies*. Random House Business Books.

166. "Middle-aged employees with little or no "peer social support" in the workplace were 2.4 times more likely to die during the study."

> Excerpt(s) from *Mastering Civility* by Christine Porath, copyright © 2016. Reprinted by permission of Grand Central Publishing, an imprint of Hachette Book Group, Inc.

167. "The American Psychology Association estimates that workplace stress costs the US economy $500 billion a year. A stunning 550 billion workdays are lost each year due to stress on the job, 60 to 80 percent of workplace accidents were because of stress, and more than 80% of doctor visits are stress related."

> Excerpt(s) from *Mastering Civility* by Christine Porath, copyright © 2016. Reprinted by permission of Grand Central Publishing, an imprint of Hachette Book Group, Inc.

168. "48% percent intentionally decreased their effort, 47 percent intentionally decreased the time spent at work, 38 percent intentionally decreased the quality of their work, 80 percent lost work time worrying about the incident, 63 percent lost work avoiding the offender, 66 percent said their performance declined, 78 percent said their commitment to the organization declined, 12 percent said they had left their job because of the uncivil treatment, and 25 percent admitted to taking their frustration out on customers... Turnover costs add up quickly: four times an employee's annual salary in the case of high-level employees."

169. "Strategy #1: Ask for focused feedback on your best and worst behaviors."

"Strategy #2: Work with a coach."

"Strategy #3: Conduct a team tune-up: use colleagues or friends as coaches."

"Strategy #4: Get 360 feedback."

"Strategy $5: Teach yourself how to read emotions."

"Strategy #6: Make time for reflection."

"Strategy #7: Take care of yourself."

170. "In fact, over 70 percent of today's employees work in an open plan…"

171. "It turns out that vertical separation is a very serious thing. If you're on a different floor in some organizations, you may as well be in a different country."

172. "Another example of the trade-off theory of evolution is a species known as Trinidadian guppies. These guppies develop personalities—with astonishing speed, in evolutionary terms—to suit the microclimates in which they live. Their natural predators are pike. But some guppy neighborhoods, upstream of a waterfall for example, are pike-free. If you're a guppy who grew up in such a charmed locale, then chances are you have a bold and carefree personality well suited to la dolce vita. In contrast, if your guppy family came from a "bad neighborhood" downstream from the waterfall, where pike cruise the waterways menacingly, then you probably have a much more circumspect style, just right for avoiding the bad guys. The interesting thing is that these differences are heritable, not learned, so that the offspring of bold guppies who move into bad neighborhoods inherit their parents' boldness—even though this puts them at a severe disadvantage compared to their vigilant peers. It doesn't take long for their genes to mutate, though, and descendants who manage to survive tend to be careful types. The same thing happens to vigilant guppies when the pike suddenly disappear; it takes about twenty years for their descendants to evolve into fish who act as if they haven't a care in the world."

173. "They discovered the weekly profits of the stores managed by extroverts were 16 percent higher than the profits of those led by introverts – but only when the employees were passive types who tended to do their job without exercising

initiative. Introverted leaders had the exact opposite results. When they worked with employees who actively tried to improve work procedures, their stores outperformed those led by extroverts by more than 14 percent. [...] When the followers were not proactive, though-when they simply did as the leader instructed-the teams led by extroverts outperformed those led by the introverts by 22 percent... But with their natural ability to inspire, extroverted leaders are better at getting results from more passive workers."

174. "In PCM there are six personality types: Thinkers, Persisters, Harmonizers, Imaginers, Rebels, and Promoters. Each personality type experiences the world in different ways. Thinkers perceive the world through thoughts, and logic is their currency. Persisters perceive the world through opinions, and value is their currency. Harmonizers perceive the world through emotions, and compassion is their currency. Imaginers perceive the world through inactions, and reactions, and humor is their currency. And last, but certainly not least, since they are often very powerful people, Promoters and they perceive the world through actions, and charm is their currency."

175. "I made a list: Close physical proximity, often in circles; Profuse amounts of eye contact; Physical touch (handshakes, fist bumps, hugs); Lots of short, energetic exchanges (no long speeches); High levels of mixing; everyone talks to everyone; Few interruptions; Lots of questions; Intensive, active listening; Humor, laughter; Small, attentive courtesies (thank-you, opening doors, etc.)"

176. "We can measure its impact on the bottom line. (A strong culture increases net income 765 percent over ten years, according to a Harvard study of more than 200 companies."

177. "Here Horowitz is out to persuade readers to adopt his experiential view that the most robust, sustainable cultures are those based on action, not words; an alignment of personality and strategy;"

> ... from *What You Do Is Who You Are* by Ben Horowitz, Copyright © 2019 by Ben Horowitz. Used by Permission of HarperCollins Publishers.

"Because your culture is how your company makes decisions when you're not there."

> ... from *What You Do Is Who You Are* by Ben Horowitz, Copyright © 2019 by Ben Horowitz. Used by Permission of HarperCollins Publishers.

"Cultural behaviors, once absorbed, get deployed everywhere."

> ... from *What You Do Is Who You Are* by Ben Horowitz, Copyright © 2019 by Ben Horowitz. Used by Permission of HarperCollins Publishers.

178. "There is a concept in cognitive psychology called the channel capacity, which refers to the amount of space in our brain for certain kinds of information."

> Excerpt(s) from *The Tipping Point*: How Little Things Can Make a Big Difference by Malcolm Gladwell, copyright © 2000. Reprinted by permission of Back Bay Books, an imprint of Hachette Book Group, Inc.

"The Rule of 150 suggests that the size of a group is another one of those subtle contextual factors that can make a big difference."

> Excerpt(s) from *The Tipping Point*: How Little Things Can Make a Big Difference by Malcolm Gladwell, copyright © 2000. Reprinted by permission of Back Bay Books, an imprint of Hachette Book Group, Inc.

179. "I explain that any organization that really wants to maximize its success must come to embody two basic qualities: it must be smart, and it must be healthy."

> Lencioni, P. (2012). *The advantage: Why organizational health trumps everything else in business*. Jossey-Bass. Printed by permission purchased through Wiley and Sons.

180. "Smart organizations are good at those classic fundamentals of business – subjects like strategy, marketing, finance, and technology – which I consider to be decision sciences."

Lencioni, P. (2012). *The advantage: Why organizational health trumps everything else in business.* Jossey-Bass. Printed by permission purchased through Wiley and Sons.

181. "A good way to recognize health is to look for the signs that indicate an organization has it. These include minimal politics and confusion, high degrees of morale and productivity, and very low turnover among good employees."

Lencioni, P. (2012). *The advantage: Why organizational health trumps everything else in business.* Jossey-Bass. Printed by permission purchased through Wiley and Sons.

182. "Discipline 1: Build a cohesive leadership team... Discipline 2: Create clarity... Discipline 3: Overcommunicate clarity... Discipline 4: Reinforce clarity."

Lencioni, P. (2012). *The advantage: Why organizational health trumps everything else in business.* Jossey-Bass. Printed by permission purchased through Wiley and Sons.

183. "When it comes to discussions and decision making, there are two critical ways that members of effective teams must communicate: advocacy and inquiry... Advocacy is the kind of communication that most people are accustomed to, and it is all about stating your case or making your point... Inquiry is rarer and more important than advocacy. It happens when people ask questions to seek clarity about another person's statement of advocacy."

Lencioni, P. (2012). *The advantage: Why organizational health trumps everything else in business.* Jossey-Bass. Printed by permission purchased through Wiley and Sons.

184. Lencioni, P. (2012). *The advantage: Why organizational health trumps everything else in business.* Jossey-Bass. Printed by permission purchased through Wiley and Sons.

185. "1. Why do we exist?... 2. How do we behave?... 3. What do we do?... 4. How will we succeed?... 5. What is important right now?... 6. Who must do what?"

Lencioni, P. (2012). *The advantage: Why organizational health trumps everything else in business.* Jossey-Bass. Printed by permission purchased through Wiley and Sons.

186. "In a project code-named Project Aristotle, Google set out to create the perfect team. The project, which studied 180 teams for two years, was given its moniker after Aristotle's famous quote "The whole is greater than the sum of its parts." [...] Ultimately, Project Aristotle identified five keys to a great team: something psychologists call psychological safety, dependability, structure and clarity around goals and roles, the discovery of personal meaning in work, and the belief that the

work the team is doing matters… Psychological safety is a climate in which people feel safe to speak up and take interpersonal risks."

Excerpt(s) from *Social Chemistry: Decoding the patterns of human connection* by Marissa King, copyright © 2020 by Marissa King. Used by permission of Dutton, an imprint of Penguin Publishing Gruoop, a division of Penguin Random House LLC. All rights reserved.

187. "This isn't all that surprising given that convening networks are safe and imbued with trust. But trust and psychological safety aren't the same thing. While they are related, trust is about a relationship between two people or two parties… Psychological safety is about the group… Trust is also about the future… Psychological safety is an immediate experience."

Excerpt(s) from *Social Chemistry: Decoding the patterns of human connection* by Marissa King, copyright © 2020 by Marissa King. Used by permission of Dutton, an imprint of Penguin Publishing Gruoop, a division of Penguin Random House LLC. All rights reserved.

188. Pink, D. (2019). *When: The scientific secrets of perfect timing.* Riverhead Books.

189. "When so many millennials entered the job market, it was either in complete shambles or in very, very slow recovery. Between December 2007 and October 2009, the unemployment rate doubled: from 5 to 10 percent. Total employment dropped by 8.6 million. And while a major nationwide recession affects nearly everyone, in some way, it especially affects those on the market for the first time. When millions of experienced workers lost their jobs, they went looking for new ones wherever they could: including the lower-paying, entry-level work where first-time job seekers generally find a foothold in the market. For millennials between sixteen and twenty-four, the unemployment rate rose from 10.8 percent in November 2007 to 19.5 percent in April 2010—a record high. […] They "graduated into the worst job market in eighty years. That did not just mean a few years of high unemployment, or a couple of years living in their parents' basements. It meant a full decade of lost wages." The extent of the effects of this timing is only now coming into focus: A 2018 report issued by the Federal Reserve, for example, found that "millennials are less well off than members of earlier generations when they were young, with lower earnings, fewer assets, and less wealth."

Petersen, A. H. (2021). *CAN'T EVEN: How millennials became the burnout generation.* Mariner Books.

190. "The Two Pillars of Happiness. The total fulfillment of one's potentialities, which usually generates happiness, depends on the simultaneous presence of two processes. It is much easier to achieve happiniess if one understands how these work. The first

is the process of differentiation, which involves realizing that we are unique individuals, responsible for our own survival and well-being, who are willing to develop this uniqueness wherever it leads, while enjoying the expression of our being in action. The second process involves integration, or the realization that however unique we are, we are also completely enmeshed in networks of relationships with other human beings, with cultural symbols and artifacts, and with the surrounding natural envinroment."

191. "1. Goals Are Clear. For a person to become deeply involved in any activity it is essential that he know precisely what tasks he must accomplish, moment by moment. [...] 2. Feedback Is Immediate. It is difficult for people to stay absorbed in any activity unless they get timely, "online" information about how well they are doing. [...] 3. A Balance Between Opportunity and Capacity. It is easier to become completely involved in a task if we believe it is doable... Flow occurs when both challenges and skills are high and equal to each other. [...] 4. Concentration Deepens. When we begin to respond to an opportunity that has clear goals and provides immediate feedback, we are likely to become involved int it, even if the activity itself is not very "important"—such as a game, a hobby, or a stimulating conversation... Concentration in flow can be so deep that the term "ecstasy" is sometimes used to describe it. In Greek ecstasy meant literally "to stand to the side." [...] 5. The Present is What Matters. Because in flow the task at hand demands complete attention, the worries and problems that are so nagging in everyday life have no chance to register in the mind. [...] 6. Control Is No Problem. When people describe their flow experiences, one of the first things they mention is a strong sens of beging in control of the situation. [...] 7. The Sense of Time Is Altered. One typical element of the flow experience is that time is experienced differently. Quite often, this means that time is percieved as flying by. [...] 8. The Loss of Ego. Many of the descriptions of flow quoted up to now have mentioned the fact that while immersed in the experience one tends to forget not only one's problems and surroundings, but one's very self."

192. "Something that is worth doing for its own sake is called autotelic (from the Greek auto = self and telos = goal), because it contains its goal within itself. We don't need

external rewards to pursue such activities; we don't require payment or admiration to play the guitar, hike in the woods, or read a good novel. Another way to term such activities is intrinsically rewarding, because their primary reward is simply in being involved with them. Contrast these with activities that are primarily exotelic or extrinsically rewarding, which we do only with the expectation of some gain, or to avoid being punished."

193. Figure 1: "Figure 2: The Map of Everyday Experience" from Good Business: Leadership Flow, and the Making of Meaning by Mihaly Csikszentmihalyi, copyright © 2003 by Mihaly Csikszentmihalyi. Used by permission of Viking Books, an imprint of Penguin Publishing Group, a Division of Penguin Random House LLC. All rights reserved.

194. Figure 1: "Figure 2: The Map of Everyday Experience" from Good Business: Leadership Flow, and the Making of Meaning by Mihaly Csikszentmihalyi, copyright © 2003 by Mihaly Csikszentmihalyi. Used by permission of Viking Books, an imprint of Penguin Publishing Group, a Division of Penguin Random House LLC. All rights reserved.

195. Figure 1: "Figure 2: The Map of Everyday Experience" from Good Business: Leadership Flow, and the Making of Meaning by Mihaly Csikszentmihalyi, copyright © 2003 by Mihaly Csikszentmihalyi. Used by permission of Viking Books, an imprint of Penguin Publishing Group, a Division of Penguin Random House LLC. All rights reserved.

196. Figure 1: "Figure 2: The Map of Everyday Experience" from Good Business: Leadership Flow, and the Making of Meaning by Mihaly Csikszentmihalyi, copyright © 2003 by Mihaly Csikszentmihalyi. Used by permission of Viking Books, an imprint of Penguin Publishing Group, a Division of Penguin Random House LLC. All rights reserved.

197. (Collins & Porras, 2005)

198. "But more and more companies began to offer nothing at all. In 1980, 46 percent of private-sector workers were covered by a pension plan. In 2019, that number had fallen to 16 percent.17 A Pew Charitable Trusts analysis of data from the 2012 Survey of Income and Program Participation found that 53 percent of private sector

employees had access to a "defined contribution" plan, like a 401k or a Roth 401k IRA. And while many celebrate the ability to move from job to job instead of sticking with an employer simply to maximize pension benefits, that flexibility creates significant 401k "leakage": employees forget to roll over a 401k, or withdraw it to cover "hardship" expenses, from college tuition to medical emergencies.18 And access to a plan is different from participation: Only 38 percent of private sector workers actually enrolled in offered defined contribution plans. It's difficult, after all, to force yourself to save for future security when your present feels so incredibly insecure."

Petersen, A. H. (2021). *CAN'T EVEN: How millennials became the burnout generation.* Mariner Books.

199. "As already noted, if one evaluates the system through a generational return-on-investment lens, Social Security has been all downhill since Ida's day. Back when the program first started, 42 workers were making contributions for every retiree drawing benefits... It is currently a bit under 3 to 1 and is slated to drop below 2 to 1 by 2035... Fifty years ago, the government spent $3 on public investments that spur economic activity for every $1 it spent on entitlements. Today that ratio has flipped, and within a decade the government will be putting $5 into entitlements for every $1 that goes to roads, education, scientific research, and the like, according to an analysis by Third Way, a centrist public policy think tank."

From *The Next America* by Paul Taylor, copyright © 2013. Reprinted by permission of Public Affairs, an imprint of Hatchette Book Group, Inc.

200. "... US respondents finished a bit above the middle of the pack, with more than 6 in 10 saying they are very (24%) or somewhat (39%) confident."

From *The Next America* by Paul Taylor, copyright © 2013. Reprinted by permission of Public Affairs, an imprint of Hatchette Book Group, Inc.

201. "In the modern era, life expectancy at birth in the US has been increasing by about a year every six years. The typical American baby born today can expect to live an average of 78.7 years, up from 75.4 years two decades ago. ... During the same two-decade period, the number of centenarians in the US grew by about 50%, to more than 50,000. By the middle of this century, according to Census Bureau forecasts, close to a half million people in the US will be at least 100 years old."

From *The Next America* by Paul Taylor, copyright © 2013. Reprinted by permission of Public Affairs, an imprint of Hatchette Book Group, Inc.

202. "Within the G6, the US is projected to see an increase in the old-age dependency ratio, from 19 in 2010 to 36 in 2050."

203. "In the US, for example, labor force participation among those 65 and older has risen from a low of 10.8% in 1985 to 18.5% in 2012, according to the Bureau of Labor Statistics."

204. "Moreover, when one looks at wealth rather than income, the gaps since the 1980s have ballooned into chasms and are starkly aligned with race and age. As of 2011, the typical white household had 14 times the wealth of the typical black household (up from 7 times in the mid-1990s) and the typical older household had 26 times the wealth of the typical younger household (up from 10 times in the mid-1980s)."

205. "In short, compound interest is earning interest on interest."

206. "Your money needs to keep up with inflation, especially when you're saving for long-term goals like retirement. [...] The earlier you start, the longer you have to let compound interest do its job for you, and the better you can weather the ups and downs of the market. And best of all, the less money you have to invest each year to meet your goal."

207. ASSET CLASS: An asset class is a grouping of similar investments. [...] PORTFOLIO: The term used to refer to your investments or the grouping of your investments. [...] PUBLIC OR PUBLICLY TRADED: When a company "goes public," that means it is no longer just owned solely by the creator of the company or

215

a close inner circle of friends, family, or venture capitalists. Now it is publicly available for the general public to buy a piece of the company by purchasing stock. [...] EQUITIES/STOCK: Here's a fun quirk: equities, stock, and shares are often used interchangeably. Equities and stock can be used as synonyms. [...] SHARES: Shares are what your stock is divided into. [...] SHAREHOLDER AND STOCKHOLDER: Shareholder and stockholder mean essentially the same thing: you own shares of a company's stock. [...] SECURITIES: You will also hear the term security or securities used to describe holding equities (stocks) and debts (bonds, certificates of deposits, etc.). [...] BONDS: You own a piece of a corporation's or government's debt when you buy a bond. [...] Ultimately, the borrower will then repay the full debt to the bondholder once the agreed-upon term is up (known as "maturity"). [...] FIXED INCOME: Fixed income investments are typically considered conservative investments because you can expect a set influx of cash. [...] CASH AND CASH EQUIVALENTS: I'm sure you get the cash part, that money in your checking account and savings account. The money you can easily access today. [...] Asset allocation is the process of deciding in which asset classes you should be investing and how much of your portfolio should go into each. [...] Diversification is best described with the cliché "Don't put all your eggs in one basket." [...] RISK TOLERANCE: This is the gut reaction you feel about the potential of losing money. [...] In the case of investing, a broker is the person (or firm) that buys and sells investments on your behalf in exchange for a fee or commission. [...] SECTORS: Sectors are industries, such as health care, energy, tech, real estate, or utilities. [...] TIME HORIZON: "What's your time horizon?" is just a fancy way of asking "When do you need the money?" [...] BROKERAGE ACCOUNT: A brokerage account is where you deposit the money you want to invest. [...] A professional, known as a portfolio or fund manager, is managing the investments directly by making decisions about when to buy, hold, and sell the investments within a fund. [...] ROI will generally refer to how much you make on your investment relative to its cost. [...] MUTUAL FUND: You give your money to a professional who pools it with strangers' money in order to buy investments. [...] EXCHANGE-TRADED FUND (ETF): A hybrid option between mutual-fund investing and being able to buy and sell stocks. [...] DIVIDEND: A payment you get from the company or fund in which you invested for being a shareholder. [...] DIVIDEND REINVESTMENT PLAN (DRIP): Instead of taking your cash dividend as a check or direct deposit into your bank account, you can use it to buy more shares."

208. Morgan, Jacob. *The Employee Experience Advantage: How to win the war for talent by giving employees the workspaces they want, the tools they need, and a culture they can celebrate.* Wiley. 2017.

209. Morgan, Jacob. *The Employee Experience Advantage: How to win the war for talent by giving employees the workspaces they want, the tools they need, and a culture they can celebrate.* Wiley. 2017.

210. Morgan, Jacob. *The Employee Experience Advantage: How to win the war for talent by giving employees the workspaces they want, the tools they need, and a culture they can celebrate.* Wiley. 2017.

211. Morgan, Jacob. *The Employee Experience Advantage: How to win the war for talent by giving employees the workspaces they want, the tools they need, and a culture they can celebrate.* Wiley. 2017.

Notes

Notes

Notes

Notes

Notes

Notes